AEROFILMS GUIDE

# The South Devon Coast Path

Des Hannigan

IAN ALLAN Publishing

# THE SOUTH DEVON COAST PATH

Based on an original idea by
Richard Cox of Aerofilms

Designer Michael D. Stride
Series Editor Rebecca King

Published by Ian Allan Ltd, Shepperton, Surrey;
and printed by Ian Allan Printing Ltd at their
works at Coombelands in Runnymede, England

Text © Ian Allan Ltd 1992
Photographs © Aerofilms 1992
(unless otherwise credited)

The publishers gratefully acknowledge the
AA Photo Library for the use of the
photograph on pages 4-5

While every effort has been taken to ensure
the accuracy of the information in this
book, the publishers cannot accept
responsibility for errors or omissions, or for
changes in details given.

First published 1992

ISBN 0 7110 2041 8

# Contents

## THE ROUTE

## FEATURES

*Inset: Axmouth*
*Main picture: Slapton Sands*
*Title page: Limpet Rocks, Torcross*

Other titles in this series:
**The South Downs Way**
**The Cotswold Way**

## *Followin*

The Countryside Commission's long-distance route symbol is an acorn and by and large waymarking along the South Devon Coast Path is good.

### OBLIQUE PHOTOGRAPHS

These photographs bring a new perspective to the landscape and its buildings. All the subjects chosen can either be seen from, lie on, or are within easy reach of the Way.

### VERTICAL PHOTO-MAPS

Every step of the Coast Path is plotted on vertical photographs using a scale of 1:10,000 (1 mile:6.5in, 1km:10cm).

### SYMBOLS

The following symbols appear on the photo-maps for information and to help the walker get his bearings.

|   |   |
|---|---|
| 🚂 | Railway station |
| ☀ | Viewpoint |
| ★ | Place of interest |
| ♟ | Pub or hotel |
| P | Car park |
| ♜ | Church |
| Ⓡ | Refreshments |

### SCALE FOR PHOTO-MAPS

The scale-bar represents a distance of 0.310 miles (0.5km).

112

The vertical photography used in the photo-maps is taken from an average height above sea level. This means that the scale of the photography will alter slightly as the contours of the ground vary. The photo-maps are constructed by piecing together a series of photographs to make each page. They are intended to give a

# 1e Route

he acorn symbol may be found on indicator plinths
r wooden signposts, or it may be stamped on a
ost or stile.

## alcombe to Bigbury-on-Sea

miles (17.6km)

exhilarating walk along the lofty heights of Bolt from `Head' to
il', through some of the most spectacular cliff scenery on the
uth Devon coast. The River Avon poses a challenge if the
asonal ferry is not running, but a way round is available if
ding deters the walker.

E NATIONAL TRUST property at
rpitor, Overbecks, houses a youth
tel and museum and is surrounded
a fascinating garden. The museum
s the creation of Otto Overbeck, a
ch chemist and inveterate collector.
ncludes shipping exhibits,
icultural implements and a fine
ection of British moths and
terflies.

ROUTE DIRECTIONS

**1.** Follow the narrow and stony path round the
seaward nose of Sharp Tor and below its startling
pinnacles. Go downhill to above Starehole Bay
and up the steeper slope to the summit of Bolt
Head.

**2.** Cross the rocky shoulder of Bolt Head and
continue along the cliff edge.

**3.** Follow the path alongside clifftop fields.

*Precariously placed properties above Stink
Cove - a place strikingly at odds with its
unattractive name*

N

### SECTIONS OF THE COAST PATH

The route from Lyme Regis to
Plymouth has been divided
into sections that can
comfortably be walked in a
day. Each of these sections
opens with an introduction
and the distance involved is
given.

### ROUTE DIRECTIONS

These numbered route
directions correspond to the
numbers shown in yellow on
the photo-maps. Sometimes
alternative paths or optional
diversions are given.

### GENERAL TEXT

Places to visit, points of
specific interest and
information relevant to that
particular stretch of the route
accompanies every photo-
map. The West Country
Tourist Boards (see page 144)
will supply opening times to
places to visit, and it is always
advisable to check details in
advance of a visit to avoid
disappointment. Generally,
opening times between
October and Easter are very
limited.

### COMPASS POINT

Every photo-map is
accompanied by a compass
point for ease of orientation.

*pictorial representation* of the ground and strict accuracy of scale
throughout cannot be guaranteed. There may also be a mismatch
in areas of extreme relief – ie where the land is steepest. These
problems have been kept to a minimum, in particular close to the
main route of the walk.

# Practical Information

## ACCOMMODATION
There are excellent hotels and guesthouses in all the main towns along the route, and bed and breakfast facilities are usually available both in the towns and in the more remote villages near the coast. Camp sites are also located at most of the larger towns.

There are youth hostels along the coast at Beer, Strete, Sharpitor and Plymouth, and at Maypool, which lies on the River Dart about 1½ miles (2.4km) south-west of Galmpton on the A3022.

It is as well to remember that accommodation is often at a premium during the summer season and advance booking may be necessary. Some premises close during the winter months, but this is balanced by the fact that there is less pressure on those remaining open.

Detailed information about accommodation of all kinds is available from the West Country Tourist Board (see page 144).

## TRANSPORT
British Rail's InterCity service runs from all parts of the country to Exeter and Plymouth and there are main line stations at Dawlish Warren, Dawlish and Teignmouth. Branch lines run from Exeter to Exmouth and from Newton Abbot to Torquay and Paignton. From Paignton to Kingswear the line is operated by the Dart Valley Railway Company, using steam trains.

National Express coaches operate from all parts of the country to the main centres from where local bus connections can be made to many coastal points. Bus information can be obtained from local tourist information centres, but note that some of these close during the winter.

## RIVER CROSSINGS
Crossings of the Exe, Teign, Dart, Avon, Erme, Velam and the Kingsbridge estuary are variable and the following should be used as a guideline only. Walkers are advised to check timetables, tides and weather conditions before arriving at crossing points.
Exmouth to Starcross (Exe): seasonal. Tel 0626 862452.
Topsham to East Bank (Exe): may be variable. Tel 0392 77888.

*Beer*

Teignmouth to Shaldon (Teign): all year with seasonal variations. Tel 0626 77977.
Kingswear to Dartmouth (Dart): all year with seasonal variations. Tel 080425 342.
East Portlemouth to Salcombe (Kingsbridge estuary): all year with seasonal variations. Tel 054884 2863/2061.
Bantham to Bigbury (Avon): seasonal. Tel 0548 560593. Note: wading of the Avon is a serious undertaking, see page 120.
River Erme. There is no ferry across the Erme and it should be waded only within strict tidal limits, see page 124.
Noss Mayo to Warren Point (Yealm): July to August. Tel 0752 872189.

## COUNTRY CODE
Enjoy the countryside and respect its life and work
Guard against all risk of fire
Fasten all gates
Keep dogs under close control
Keep to public paths across farmland
Use gates and stiles to cross fences, hedges and walls
Leave livestock crops and machinery alone
Take your litter home
Help to keep all water clean
Protect wildlife, plants and trees
Take special care on country roads; keep to the right and walk in single file
Make no unnecessary noise

## RIGHTS OF WAY

There are two main kinds of public rights of way: footpaths, open to walkers only, and bridleways, open to walkers, horse-riders and bicycle-riders. Footpaths are sometimes waymarked with a yellow dot and bridleways with a blue dot. Another category is byways, or 'roads used as a public path', and these can be used by walkers, horse-riders, cyclists and motor vehicles.

It is permissible to take a pram, pushchair or wheelchair along rights of way, and a dog if kept under control. You are also entitled to make a short detour around an obstruction, or remove it in order to get past.

There are also a number of other areas to which the public are allowed access by established custom or consent, and these include country parks and picnic sites, beaches, canal towpaths, some woodlands and forests, particularly those owned by the Forestry Commission, and many areas of open country. For more information about walking and the law contact the Countryside Commission (address on page 144).

It is worth remembering that hedges and fences can be removed, rights of way re-routed, paths become very overgrown, and in wet weather conditions streams and rivers may be impassable.

*Erme estuary*

## BEFORE YOU GO

Careful planning, adequate footwear and appropriate clothing are the keys to enjoyable walking and this is particularly so as far as the South Devon Coast Path is concerned. There are a number of very steep slopes on the route and footwear with a good grip is essential. Always carry a waterproof and enough food and drink for the day ahead and allow yourself plenty of time. Optional extras might include a pair of binoculars, a good field guide or two, swimming things and a sun hat.

## AEROFILMS LIMITED

Aerofilms was founded in 1919 and has specialised in the acquisition of aerial photography within the United Kingdom throughout its history. The company has a record of being innovative in the uses and applications of aerial photography.

Photographs looking at the environment in perspective are called oblique aerial photographs. These photographs are taken with Hasselblad cameras by professional photographers experienced in the difficult conditions encountered in aerial work.

Photographs looking straight down at the landscape are termed vertical aerial photographs. These photographs are obtained by using Leica survey cameras, the products from which are normally used in the making of maps.

Aerofilms has a unique library of oblique and vertical photographs in excess of one and a half million covering the United Kingdom. This library of photographs dates from 1919 to the present and is continually being updated.

Oblique and vertical photography can be taken to customers' specification by Aerofilms' professional photographers. Due to the specific nature of the requirements of the Aerofilms guides, new photography has been taken for these books.

To discover more of the wealth of past or present photographs held in the library at Aerofilms, including photographs in this guide, or to commission new aerial photography to your requirements, please contact:

Aerofilms Limited
Gate Studios
Station Road
Borehamwood
Herts
WD6 1EJ
Telephone: 081-207 0666
Fax: 081-207 5433

# Introduction to the South Devon Coast Path

South Devon has one of the finest coasts in England and for most of its 120 or so miles (193km) it faces into the sun, sheltered from prevailing winds by the great shoulder of Dartmoor. Its eastern shore lies within the gentle curve of Lyme Bay, while the more exposed western section has all of Cornwall to bear the brunt of Atlantic weather. Hard winds and stormy seas from the south and east can still batter the Devon coast and add a salty sparkle to coastal walking, but the climate overall is benign, earning the region the title of 'English Riviera'.

The eastern chalk cliffs, draped in greenery at Beer and Branscombe, stand in striking contrast to the blood-red marl of Sidmouth's High Peak and the Dawlish coast, while the clean sweep of beaches between these sudden heights has a genuine Mediterranean flavour. Yet this is still Island Britain and the exotic nature of the landscape here is tempered further west by the great bristling headlands of Start Point, Prawle and Bolt Head, which have the dark look of Welsh mountain ridges — slate-grey and dragon-backed above a less easy sea.

In places the coast has been overpowered by development, not least along the holiday beaches of Torbay; yet here is another intriguing contrast. The bustle and excitement of the great resorts and harbours of Torquay, Paignton and Brixham is balanced by the serenity of the River Erme, by the Yealm at Noss Mayo, by the remoteness of the vast cliffs of Dunscombe and Prawle and by the green depths of the eastern Undercliffs.

This astonishing variety of scenery is available to the walker via the South Devon Coast Path and the landforms of the area ensure a vigorous mix of walking

country guaranteed to delight and
satisfy. Devon is famous for its
deep combes and those water-worn
valleys that run to the sea, cradled
between high, hump-backed cliffs,
turn sections of the Coast Path into
a giant roller-coaster. At a lower
pitch, the coast is breached by
sizeable rivers that necessitate
ferry transport, inland detours, or
carefully-considered ford
crossings.

   Many parts of the South Devon
Coast Path are satisfyingly remote,
yet nowhere is the walker more
than a few miles from all modern
services and convenient escape
points. Scattered along the coast
are the handsome towns of

Exmouth and Teignmouth,
splendid sailing centres like
Salcombe, Dartmouth and Newton
Ferrers, and lively resorts like
Torbay. In between lie such
delightful inland villages as
Branscombe, Salcombe Regis and
Otterton, and shoreline settlements
include Dawlish, Stoke Fleming,
Torcross and Bigbury. All offer the
opportunity of enjoying an
overnight stay in a delightful
setting, and what could be better
after a good day's walking through
some of the finest coastal scenery
in Europe.

_Inset: Paignton_

# Lyme Regis to Seaton

7 miles (11km)

**The coast between Lyme Regis and Seaton comprises a deeply wooded landslip area, 6 miles (9.6km) long and ½ mile (800m) wide, known as the Undercliffs. The walk through these is delightful, although a safe exit is possible from one point only. The path is well-trodden but strenuous, and uneven where gnarled tree roots have broken the surface. This stretch can be very muddy in wet conditions. Walkers should allow three to four hours for the trip, and there are no refreshment points.**

THE BREAKWATER-CUM-HARBOUR at Lyme Regis, known as the Cobb, is a unique and compelling feature. Its present form dates from the early 18th century although records go back to the medieval period. A number of historic features still survive on the Cobb and there is an interesting aquarium here.

The Cobb is famous in both classical and contemporary literature. Jane Austen set her novel *Persuasion* in Lyme Regis and used the Cobb in a dramatic scene where her heroine Louisa Musgrove falls from the higher wall. The Cobb has become even more famous in recent times through the novel *The French Lieutenant's Woman*, written by John Fowles who lives

locally. The film of the book has immortalised the image of the tragic heroine in her black cloak hauntingly alone at the seaward end of the famous breakwater.

It is tempting to linger here, but for the coastal walker the route to the west beckons through the remarkable Undercliffs landslip and within seconds the walker leaves the airy openness of the Cobb and plunges into woodland.

ROUTE DIRECTIONS

**1.** The Coast Path starts from Cobb Gate on the Lyme Regis seafront. Walk west along Marine Parade to the Cobb.

LYME REGIS

*The harbour at Lyme Regis has long since ceased to attract commercial trade, but fishing and pleasure boats continue to berth within the protective wall of the Cobb*

**2.** Go west from the Cobb past a yacht pound and car park to just beyond the Lyme Regis bowling club. Turn right through a small car park and climb some steps. Continue between wooden chalets on to a tree-shaded path. Stay on the main path.

**3.** Enter Devon above Devonshire Head, just before joining a section of surfaced track by a house. Follow the track to where it veers down left to Underhill Farm.

**4.** Follow the path that leads off the track directly into the woods and past a Nature Conservancy Council information board. It is important to keep to the path from now on. The deep undergrowth to either side masks dangerous fissures and hollows in the Undercliffs.

ABOVE UNDERHILL FARM a Nature Conservancy Council notice warns walkers that the next few miles through the Undercliffs should not be undertaken lightly. Do not be discouraged, the path is clearly defined and if plenty of time is allowed the walk through this fascinating green world is easily accomplished.

The East Devon coast is noted for spectacular landslips, but none are so extensive or impressive as this stretch. Such land formations are caused by the natural instability of the underlying rock forms and the widely differing geological layers: the surface layer is chalk, which lies on top of deep greensand. These top layers are relatively young and sprightly in geological terms, being a mere 100 million years old. They rest uneasily on a thin layer of impermeable clay known as gault which in turn lies on much older limestones, shales and mudstones formed about 150 to 200 million years ago. The gault and the older rocks slope towards the sea at an angle of roughly 5 degrees.

Geologists believe that rainwater seeps down through the upper layers of chalk and greensand, reaches the impermeable gault and runs off towards the sea. As it does so it erodes the lower layers of the greensand mass. Nature finally takes its course when the sodden upper layers are so undermined that they slide seawards down the sloping surface of gault in massive blocks. The blocks rotate back on themselves to form chaotic fissures, chasms, islanded pinnacles, plateaux and inland cliffs.

## ROUTE DIRECTIONS

**1.** The path merges with a surfaced track coming in from the right. Follow the track to a distinctive pumping station.

**2.** Turn right on to a narrow path on the west side of the pumping station to where the path broadens into a track flanked by exposed water pipes.

**3.** Reach a large tree where the pipes end and where the track divides at metal and concrete drains. Follow the track to the left of the tree for a few yards. Where it bends down to the left (there are ruins of a building among the trees) go straight ahead along a narrow overgrown path which soon widens. Go down a very steep section of stepped path to join a broad track coming in from the right.

THE UNDERCLIFFS

*The Undercliffs west of Lyme were designated a National Nature Reserve in 1955 and the dense undergrowth shelters a rich variety of wildlife*

*Allhallows School*

## ROUTE DIRECTIONS

**1.** The Coast Path reaches an open area with the ruins of a tall, red-brick chimney on the right. Leave the main track by going sharply left at a signpost a short distance beyond the ruined chimney. There is a safe exit from the Undercliffs from this point, if required: stay on the main track which leads inland to reach Allhallows School and thence the A3052.

**2.** Keep to the path as it winds through the Dowlands landslip.

**3.** Continue on the path without straying to either side to reach an open space just above the sea and below the distinctive cliff face of Goat Island.

THE DOWLANDS LANDSLIP is an impressive and well-documented example of a typical undercliff. It was formed on Christmas Eve 1839 when an estimated 8 million tons of rock slid down towards the sea. The event was genuinely cataclysmic. About ¾ mile (1.2km) of cliff-top and 20 acres (8 hectares) of field were carried down, resulting in a chaos of fissures and chasms interspersed with pinnacles and rock masses. A 40ft-high (12m) offshore ridge over a mile long was temporarily thrown up, but this soon disappeared.

Landslip areas provide a variety of undisturbed habitats and these famous Undercliffs are particularly rich in wildlife. They were once worked by rabbit trappers, pig breeders, fossil gatherers and woodsmen who made their homes in the woods. The ruined building mentioned in the previous section was known as West Cliff Cottage. Built in 1830, it was inhabited for only 10 years. Other houses were occupied well into this century, including Cliff Cottage, further west, from which two elderly ladies served teas to thirsty walkers. The derelict red-brick chimney at the track junction below Allhallows School was part of a Victorian pumphouse supplying water to the school and the inland estate.

However, for many years the Undercliffs have stood undisturbed. For the naturalist, a trip through them is at once fascinating and frustrating, trapped as the walker is by the narrow way. The tree cover includes ash, beech, sycamore, oak and alder with privet, hawthorn, sloe, maple, dogwood and crabapple contributing to the marvellous profusion of scrub. Braided tendrils of traveller's joy hang from the trees like jungle creepers. Flowering plants and herbs are prolific throughout the Undercliffs. Wild madder, honeysuckle, wood spurge and purple loosestrife fringe the path, as do many other common species. Birds are plentiful and 120 species, including seabirds and migrants, have been recorded. Blackbirds, great-spotted and green woodpeckers reside with such charmers as nightingales, goldcrests and willow warblers. Roe deer colonise the Undercliffs though they are rarely seen, while badgers, foxes and rabbits are common. In high summer, the woods throb with insect life.

THE BROAD AND FERTILE valley of
the River Axe comes as a welcome sight
on emerging from the enclosed
Undercliffs. The river, once navigable as
far as Musbury, 3 miles (4.8km) inland,
meant Seaton and Axmouth were busy
ports before the Romans came to Britain.
The river's commercial and strategic
potential, however, was greatly
expanded by the Romans. Like many
South Devon rivers, the Axe became
heavily silted and blocked by shingle, a
process hastened by the great landslips
to the east.

Seaton was immensely important in
Roman times. It was the headquarters of
the Second Legion and one branch of
the Fosse Way started here. The town is
now a modern tourist resort and
although it never acquired the
fashionable stylishness of Lyme Regis or
Sidmouth, its fine open prospect makes
it a pleasant place to stop.

*Top right:*
*Before the River Axe silted up in the*
*14th century the sleepy village of Axmouth*
*was an important port*

## ROUTE DIRECTIONS

**1.** The path veers inland to reach a stile with a Nature Conservancy Council information board just beyond. Cross a stile then turn left into a field. Follow the path along the field's edge to where it veers inland.

*2.* Go down between high hedges, then turn left at a junction with a broad track to reach a gate and stile leading on to the Axe Cliff golf course.

**3.** Cross the golf course past small footpath signs at ground level. *Beware of flying golf balls*. Go past the course clubhouse and then down a narrow surfaced lane to the B3172.

**4.** Turn left at the main road, then cross the River Axe by the old bridge. Just past the bridge go left through a wooden gate into a yacht pound, and so to the seafront. Alternatively, the seafront can be reached by walking past the wooden gate for a few yards and turning left down Trevelyan Road.

SEATON

# Seaton to Sidmouth

9 miles (14.4km)

**This is a demanding but immensely rewarding section of the walk, featuring dramatic sea cliffs punctuated by remote coves. It includes some very steep combes. After Branscombe Mouth there are no refreshment points on the Coast Path. Signposting is generally good but there are places where it may confuse.**

BEER, CUPPED BETWEEN chalk cliffs, is a delight. The name comes from the Old English word *beare*, meaning grove. It has a sheltered pebble beach with first-class facilities for bathing and there are numerous shops and services available.

Beer stone was worked from Roman times for building and the now disused Beer Quarry lies about a mile (1.6km) east of the village along Quarry Lane. There are guided tours during the season.

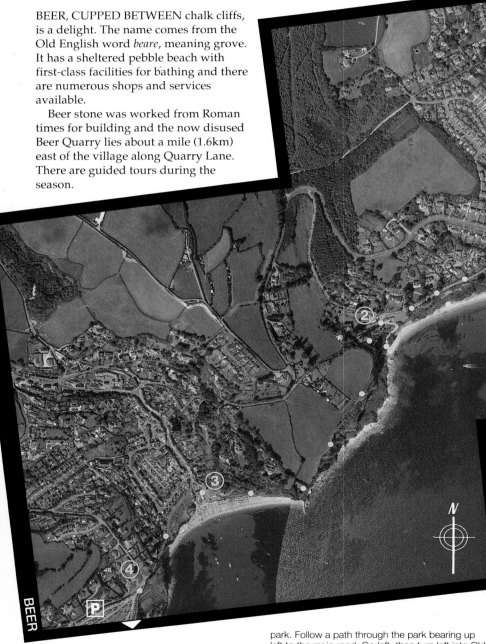

### ROUTE DIRECTIONS

**1**. Walk to the western end of Seaton promenade to where steps lead down on to the beach beyond a toilet block. At low water and during calm seas walk the short distance along the beach to Seaton Hole, where a steep road leads up to a junction with a lane. (When sea conditions are wrong for the beach crossing, go inland alongside the toilet block and up steps to a small park. Follow a path through the park bearing up left to the main road. Go left, then turn left into Old Beer Road to reach the same point above Seaton Hole.)

**2**. Walk left and uphill, then turn left up a flight of steps. Continue towards Beer keeping to the left-hand surfaced path.

**3**. Pass a children's playground above the beach at Beer, then turn left up Common Lane past a row of pebble-dash houses on the right.

**4**. Turn left by the car park at the top of Common Lane and go along Little Lane.

*Beer, a former haunt of smugglers, now caters mainly for tourists although a small fleet of fishing boats still operates from the shingle beach*

BEER HEAD, at 425ft (130m) and with its dramatic eastern cliffs enhanced by hanging curtains of greenery, is the most easterly chalk headland in England. Before reaching the Head the first feature to be encountered is a large caravan park, one of several sited close to the Coast Path throughout South Devon. Beyond here the path runs through fields amid banks and folds in the ground that indicate the land was used for agriculture in prehistoric times.

The remarkable feature known as Under Hooken is similar to the Dowlands Undercliff between Lyme and Seaton, though it is shorter and more open. The path soon presents a choice with the higher way leading on easily and unremarkably along the rim of Hooken Cliff. Few long-distance walkers, however, will be able to resist the Undercliff route where the path leads in a steep downward zig-zag, past small outcrops of pure white chalk, into the landslip beneath impressive cliffs.

Under Hooken landslip was formed in March 1790 when about 10 acres (4 hectares) of land slid down towards the sea. The area is now stabilised and is a paradise for flora and fauna, being particularly rich in insect and butterfly life during the summer. Above the land slip are impressive chalk cliffs while seaward are a number of fine pinnacles thrusting out of the undergrowth. A notable feature on the inland cliff face is a large cave-mouth said to be the end of a drainage adit (shaft) from Beer Quarry, a mile (1.6km) inland.

The path leaves the landslip through an area of pleasantly sited caravans and chalets. These occupy the formerly extremely fertile plots which, enriched with seaweed, belonged to the market gardens where the famed Branscombe broad beans and early potatoes were produced.

BEER HEAD

## ROUTE DIRECTIONS

**1**. Turn left at the edge of a caravan park, then follow a well-worn path through fields to Beer Head.

**2**. Beyond Beer Head there is a choice of paths. A stile on the left gains a path leading down into the landslip area of Under Hooken. This is the most interesting route. An easier alternative is to remain on the path along the rim of Hooken Cliff to reach

a junction from which a left turn leads down to Branscombe Mouth.

**3**. Follow the landslip path where it levels off through the thick undergrowth below high chalk cliffs.

**4**. Continue past several caravans and chalets to reach Branscombe Mouth where there are toilets, a shop and a café. Opening times are seasonal. Go inland into a field, signposted, just beyond the shop at Branscombe Mouth. Follow a rising path to a gate leading into woods.

THE CAFÉ ABOVE the attractive beach at Branscombe Mouth stands on the site of a walled coalyard. In the last century collier vessels from South Wales used to ground on the pebble beach to unload their cargo which was used to fuel a nearby gypsum mill and various lime kilns. Fishing and smuggling were the other, more romantic, sources of income.

About ½ mile (800m) inland is Branscombe itself, a delightful village with a fine old pub, The Mason's Arms, a thatched working smithy, and the splendid church of St Winifred - one of the finest in the West Country - featuring Saxon, Norman, Elizabethan and 18th century work.

The Coast Path leads from Branscombe Mouth into West Cliff, a pleasantly cool and sheltered wooded area giving charming glimpses of Branscombe village through dappled shade. (A path from the village links with the coastal path at this point.) At Berry Cliff there are remains of an embankment fortification probably dating from the Iron Age. Between Branscombe and Berry Cliff are the Branscombe Humps where the flinty ground and overgrown spoil heaps known as `rubble knapps' indicate that chalk was burnt here to produce lime.

---

ROUTE DIRECTIONS

**1**. Follow the track through West Cliff Woods. This section can be muddy in wet conditions.

**2**. Turn left down a track to reach an open area. Follow the right-hand path up and over grassy mounds and past the remains of a red-brick wall. Bear up right through a gap, then go left along the grassy edge of the cliff above a distinctive landslip area.

**3**. Go straight ahead at a signpost in the middle of an open slope. Do not go down left. The arrow pointing down left leads to a steep path down to the shore line.

**4**. Continue to a large field, turn left and follow the field's edge round to the right to the far corner, then cross a stile.

---

*Branscombe from the east. The village tumbles down the combe which emerges at Branscombe Mouth*

*Deep wooded combes such as this at Weston are a familiar feature of the South Devon coastline, and one which walkers view with mixed feelings*

WESTON MOUTH is reached down a steep slope from the summit of Weston Cliff which, at 533ft (162m), is the highest point on the South Devon coast. Weston is typical of the deep Devon combes that have been worn by streams making their way to the sea through the soft marls and chalk. Fishing and the inevitable smuggling were key activities here. The private chalets overlooking the beach were once fishermen's huts, while the small stone house set on a plinth at the western side of the beach was the customs and excise watchhouse.

Just over ¾ mile (1.2km) inland from Weston Mouth is the famous Slade Farm Donkey Sanctuary. A path leads to the Sanctuary from Weston Mouth.

The striking white cliffs above and to the west of Weston Mouth are Rempstone Rocks, the last chalk outcrops in England. They stand above yet another landslip that tumbles down to isolated shingle beaches. The path goes through another area of old chalk burnings called Dunscombe Humps, where there is a particularly striking spill of gleaming flint shards. On the slopes of Dunscombe Coppice are the quarries, now overgrown, where the lovely and easily worked Dunscombe sandstone was cut in the 14th century to build Exeter Cathedral.

## ROUTE DIRECTIONS

**1**. Follow the path through some more fields to continue along the edge of Weston Cliff.

**2**. Cross a stile at the top of a steep slope running down to Weston Mouth. *Do not follow the apparent path down the extreme edge of the cliff even though the signpost may seem to indicate this. The path is dangerous and badly overgrown.* Instead, walk a few yards to the right (inland) from the stile and follow a good stepped path that runs downhill.

**3**. At Weston Mouth go down on to the pebbled beach. Turn right and cross a small stream, then go right up a stepped path that leads very steeply to a gate and stile. Go left up to the wooden gate.

**4**. Beyond the gate continue on a steep winding path through woods. Near the top of the slope turn left at a signpost; at a junction bear right on to the cliff.

**5**. Continue past a large patch of white flinty rocks to where the path goes left down a short stepped section, then right through some trees and over a stile.

**6**. Follow the path round the rim of a small, deeply vegetated combe and continue along the seaward edge of some fields.

*Salcombe Regis nestles safely in a combe a mile or so inland; its church of St Mary and St Peter can be seen at the centre of the village*

THE WEIGHTLESS DESCENT from Dunscombe Cliff into Salcombe Mouth is marred only by sight of the formidable rise of the opposite slope!

Lying some ¾ mile (1.2km) inland is the serene little village of Salcombe Regis with its fine Norman church, the tower of which is said to have been used for storing smuggled goods, including extremely potent brandy. The name Salcombe indicates that there was once a salt factory here.

The climb uphill from Salcombe Mouth is actually quite reasonable if taken steadily. At the top there is a welcome bench with a strangely out-of-place flinty stone behind it. This is the Frogstone. It was transported to its position from Hook Ebb Reef, just east of Salcombe Mouth, by naval helicopter in 1964. This was done at the lighthearted request of the estimable Sid Vale Association. The SVA does sterling work in protecting the local environment. It was founded in 1846 and was the first Amenity Society' in Britain.

A short distance west of the Frogstone is a memorial stone to the enlightened landowner Vaughan Cornish, who dedicated the surrounding area as a permanent public open space in 1939. Through the adjoining gate there is access to a viewing platform and toposcope. From here the descent of the wooded Salcombe Hill takes a pleasant course through elder and blackthorn trees and a profusion of wild flowers in spring and early summer.

## ROUTE DIRECTIONS

**1**. Descend steeply to Salcombe Mouth. This route is difficult when wet, and an alternative zig-zag path can be taken, reducing both erosion and velocity!

**2**. Turn inland at the bottom of a field and reach a signpost. Go left over a footbridge into a field (a path to the right leads to Salcombe Regis). Turn left to reach a signpost at the seaward corner of the field from where Salcombe Mouth Beach can be reached via a steep path and steps.

**3**. Turn right and climb steeply uphill to reach the Frogstone.

**4**. Go through a gate by the Vaughan Cornish memorial stone to an open space. Take the middle one of three broad tracks down to a signpost by a wooden bench. Turn left and go down through trees to reach Sidmouth via the Alma bridge.

# SIDMOUTH

Sidmouth has been blessed with continuity of civic pride since it developed as a stylish Regency resort in the 19th century. The result is a town of great architectural interest which has been sympathetically modernised: hundreds of listed buildings contribute to the town's genteel yet unfaded charm.

The town developed inland along the banks of the River Sid and lies framed handsomely between the great red cliffs of Salcombe Hill and Peak Hill. Like its coastal neighbours to east and west, the town was originally a fishing village. There is evidence that the coast to the west of modern Sidmouth once extended much farther to seaward and provided a sheltered anchorage. Boats were built on the foreshore and the town was noted for its seafarers.

Sidmouth fishermen pursued pilchard and mackerel as far as Land's End as well as to the North Sea, while Sidmouth boats sailed the Atlantic to join the famous Grand Banks cod fishery off Newfoundland. The powerful tradition of Sidmouth seafaring and boat-building is maintained by the present-day fishing fleet with its clinker-built boats, and by the modern sailing displays and races which delight visitors.

The inevitable decline of Sidmouth's traditional industries left the town directionless until the fashionable gentry discovered its delights in the late 18th century. As with Lyme Regis, the Napoleonic wars discouraged the wealthy from wintering in France and fuelled their desire to find a safer alternative in England. Sidmouth fitted the bill as a fashionable and temperate watering place because of its mild

*Sidmouth's mile-long esplanade is backed by elegant Georgian and Regency houses*

climate, generally amenable seas and lush Devon hinterland. It was patronised by the wealthy merchant class, by the titled and by royalty. Queen Victoria came to Sidmouth as a child with her parents and her son, the Duke of Connaught, was a regular and popular patron - and Elizabeth Barrett Browning also visited.

The gentry brought with them their own ideas and fashions in house building and the town soon acquired handsome buildings whose Georgian and Regency styles give Sidmouth its distinction. Many families built themselves handsome villas, some of a peculiarly Doric cast and many of them thatched. The characteristic lace work balconies that still grace the seafront buildings were introduced, as was the fashionable chinoiserie pagoda-style roof. English fashion's ability to absorb the exotic is wonderfully illustrated at Sidmouth.

The town should not be bypassed too quickly, even at the height of the season. Sidmouth contrasts nicely with Lyme Regis in its open-fronted out look and in the comfortable spread of its streets. It is a pleasure to browse through before once more heading west up Peak Hill, described by one 18th century visitor as 'a mountain almost perpendicular . . .', though to the modern walker, a mere stroll.

# Sidmouth to Budleigh Salterton

6 miles (9.6km)

This section of the Coast Path is much less strenuous
than the last.  It involves a few inclines but
generally runs along the level rim of cliffs
which steadily decline in height towards
Budleigh Salterton.  Refreshments and
toilets are available during the
season at the halfway stage of
Ladram Bay from where
Otterton and the A376
can easily be reached.

*Sidmouth's elegant
esplanade gives way
to the red cliffs of
Peak Hill to the west*

THE GRASSY WALKWAY, liberally
supplied with memorial seats, which
sweeps away from Connaught Gardens
is a pleasure to follow. The cliff path is
soon regained and leads on to Peak Hill
from where splendid
views to the west
show High Peak's graceful sweep of red
marl cliff and the Big Picket Rock at its
base.

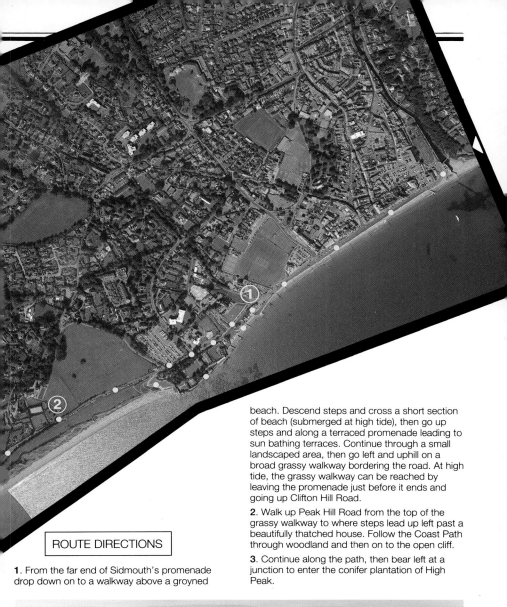

beach. Descend steps and cross a short section of beach (submerged at high tide), then go up steps and along a terraced promenade leading to sun bathing terraces. Continue through a small landscaped area, then go left and uphill on a broad grassy walkway bordering the road. At high tide, the grassy walkway can be reached by leaving the promenade just before it ends and going up Clifton Hill Road.

**2**. Walk up Peak Hill Road from the top of the grassy walkway to where steps lead up left past a beautifully thatched house. Follow the Coast Path through woodland and then on to the open cliff.

**3**. Continue along the path, then bear left at a junction to enter the conifer plantation of High Peak.

## ROUTE DIRECTIONS

**1**. From the far end of Sidmouth's promenade drop down on to a walkway above a groyned

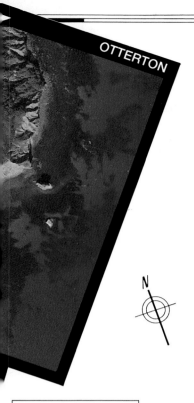

OTTERTON

THE OFFSHORE sea stacks at Ladram Bay are a famous feature of Devon's south coast. The best example is Big Picket Rock nestling at the base of High Peak to the east. Within the Bay itself are a number of fine wind-sculpted pinnacles. Ladram Bay is a place of uneasy contrasts with its unspoiled coastal scenery and its seasonally busy caravan park crowding the approach. In Victorian times the small beaches were the nude bathing preserve of 'gentlemen'. Before then they were well-used by well-dressed smugglers.

Otterton, one of Devon's loveliest villages, can be reached from Ladram Bay by walking up Bay Road then turning left down Ladram Road, a distance of about ¾ mile (1.2km). A small tributary of the River Otter runs down Otterton's main street in an open culvert and there are some fine cob and thatched roof cottages, plus a pub. Ancient Otterton Mill has been restored and is open to the public. It produces stone ground flour and there are accompanying craft workshops.

Less than a mile (1.6km) north-west of Otterton is Bicton Park, which has extensive gardens and a countryside museum, plus a host of other attractions.

N

## ROUTE DIRECTIONS

**1**. Follow a broad and level path through the trees. The summit of High Peak with its splendid views can be reached by diverting on to a narrow path running up left.

**2**. At Ladram Bay, where there is a seasonal café, a shop, toilets and telephone, cross in front of a pub to reach a lane leading down to a small beach. Go right up the lane for a short distance, then left at a signpost into a field. Follow the path along the inland edge of the field to cross a plank bridge.

**3**. Follow the path as it runs along the cliff edge with wide fields on the right.

*A footpath from Otterton leads to Bicton Park, where gardens, glasshouses and a countryside museum can be found. The open-air arena nearby is used to stage all manner of equestrian events*

THE CLIFFS west of Ladram are lower in height than the spectacular High Peak. This is a lonely stretch of coast, well-used by smugglers in the great days of the trade and the name Brandy Head speaks for itself. Chiselbury Bay, next to Ladram, was a favourite landing place for smuggled goods. The trade was supported by the gentry and even clerics. The vicars of East Budleigh were closely involved with smuggling from the mid-17th century to the mid-18th, and the vicarage was the headquarters and hiding place for the local gangs.

The River Otter was navigable as far as Otterton until the mid-15th century. Anchoring Hill, above the village, was so-named when fishing boats and small cargo vessels berthed there. East Budleigh and Budleigh Haven were also busy 'ports' from which wool was exported. Silting of the river increased

due to the formation of the shingle banks along the seashore, while a possible uplift in the general land surface may also have contributed.

The Otter now winds its sinuous way through a fine nature reserve of mudflats and reed beds under the care of the Devon Wildlife Trust. Estuarine birds include waders and shelducks, with cormorants and other seabirds also present. A sizeable flock of Canada geese frequent the Otter and make an impressive sight in the air, plus a lot of noise.

ROUTE DIRECTIONS

**1**. Follow the path above Twopenny Loaf Rock and past a derelict look-out used during the last war.

**2**. Continue above steep red cliffs at Brandy Head and Black Head to where the path descends a field edge to the River Otter.

**3**. The Otter should not be waded under any circumstances. It is deep, tidal and fast flowing. From the east bank follow the path inland passing a bird hide. Cross a small footbridge below South Farm.

**4**. Turn left at the road, cross a bridge,then turn left and follow the well-worn path down the west bank of the river to reach the large car park at Budleigh Salterton.

*The sheer cliffs of Crab Ledge*

BUDLEIGH SALTERTON takes its intriguing name from an ancient chieftain and a pinch of simple salt. Early sources give the name Saltre, later modified to Saltern - a reference to the salt pans once worked at the Otter's mouth. When the Otter ceased to be fully navigable the town survived for many years on salt processing, fishing and, of course, smuggling. The seas hereabouts were well-used by smugglers for sinking rafts of brandy tubs for later retrieval.

After the Napoleonic wars fashionable visitors descended on Budleigh Salterton in their search for home-grown equivalents to French watering places and the town took on a new persona to match its mainly 19th century architecture. Today, it retains a subdued charm.

There is a long, curving shingle beach and a fine open prospect to the sea that once absorbed the young Walter Raleigh who was born at nearby Hayes Barton. The famous painting, *The Boyhood of Raleigh*, was set by Sir John Millais against Budleigh's sea wall. Millais used his two sons and the river ferryman as models.

The story of the town is revealed in an interesting Arts Centre and Museum in a thatched building in Fore Street.

The Coast Path west of Budleigh Salterton leads pleasantly uphill and on to the wooded heights of West Down. A wire fence separates the East Devon golf club's manicured greens from the marvellous tangle of the seaward undergrowth. The golf club was laid out by a leading local family, the Rolles.

### ROUTE DIRECTIONS

**1**. Follow the promenade to its western end. Ignore the road veering off right into the town. Instead, continue alongside the beach then go uphill on a surfaced walkway.

**2**. Continue along narrow alley-ways between houses to reach an open field. Keep to its left edge.

**3**. Follow the path through woodland and alongside the wire fence of a golf course.

*Budleigh Salterton's beach stretches for nearly 2 miles (3.2km) in an absolutely straight line between Otterton Ledge and Littleham Cove*

# Budleigh Salterton to Topsham

8 miles (12.8km)

**From Straight Point onwards the walker rejoins 'civilisation' of a sort. In summer especially the masses of holiday-makers in and around Exmouth and the bustle of the Exe estuary contrast sharply with the remoter stretches of the route already covered. One compensation is the easier walking, although regaining the true coast on the western shores of the Exe estuary can be awkward.**

*Marred by an enormous caravan site and rifle ranges these days, Straight Point separates the popular beaches of Littleham Cove (east) and Sandy Bay*

THE COAST PATH
descends from West Down Beacon towards the rather overpowering Sandy Bay caravan park, which is one of the largest on Devon's south coast. The path initially runs above an area of extensive landslip cliffs known as The Floors - best viewed by a backward glance from above Littleham Cove at the start of the caravan park. The Coast Path then threads its rather fraught way between the caravan complex and the off-limits Royal Marine rifle range on Straight Point.

Sandy Bay is just what the name implies, and is the first sizeable stretch of true sandy beach encountered since the Dorset border. It is well-spoken-for during the season since it serves the adjoining caravan park.

## ROUTE DIRECTIONS

**1**. From West Down Beacon follow the path downhill through gorse and then along the edges of fields to cross a footbridge in a wooded dell.

**2**. Keep close to the cliff edge above Littleham Cove on entering the caravan park. Keep left to cross a gravelled area between caravans and the rifle range perimeter, then go up a grassy slope to a high hedge and a signpost.

**3**. Turn right and follow the path to the rim of Sandy Bay. Here there is a seasonal shop, refreshments, toilets and a telephone.

**4**. Go uphill above the beach to enter the National Trust property of High Land of Orcombe. Continue along the flat seaward edge of fields to reach Orcombe Point.

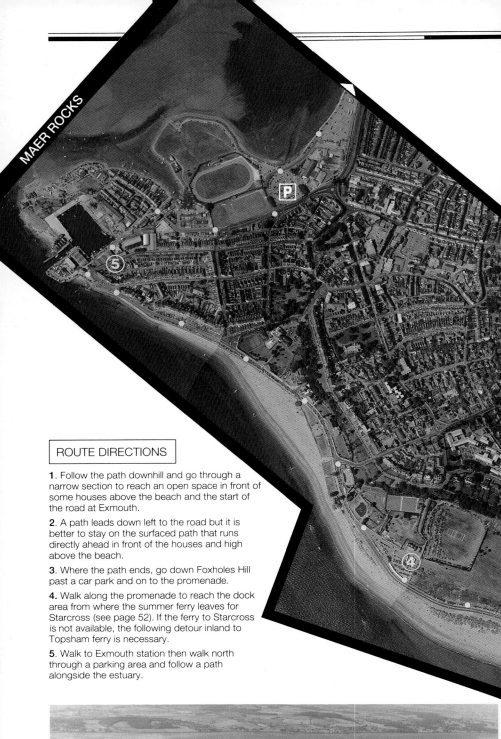

MAER ROCKS

## ROUTE DIRECTIONS

**1**. Follow the path downhill and go through a narrow section to reach an open space in front of some houses above the beach and the start of the road at Exmouth.

**2**. A path leads down left to the road but it is better to stay on the surfaced path that runs directly ahead in front of the houses and high above the beach.

**3**. Where the path ends, go down Foxholes Hill past a car park and on to the promenade.

**4**. Walk along the promenade to reach the dock area from where the summer ferry leaves for Starcross (see page 52). If the ferry to Starcross is not available, the following detour inland to Topsham ferry is necessary.

**5**. Walk to Exmouth station then walk north through a parking area and follow a path alongside the estuary.

JUST INLAND from the High Land of Orcombe lies the village of Littleham. It has an interesting church with several memorials to the Drake family in the churchyard, and here too is the grave of Lady Nelson, the wife of Horatio Nelson and by far the saddest figure in a famous love triangle. Nelson showed a deep fondness for his wife for nearly a dozen years of marriage until his notorious affair with Emma Hamilton. The marriage was childless and when her rival bore the Admiral a daughter and called her Horatia, years of silent suffering by Lady Nelson ended in public separation and rancour.

Beyond Orcombe Point the Coast Path makes its way to the great estuary of the River Exe. From the Point the view is imposing, with the river's mouth seemingly unfordable. The Exe floods out across its great swathes of tidal sand that lie banked up along the foreshore from Rodney Point and The Maer, and along the length of Exmouth's sprawling, breezy promenade. On this eastern shore lies the deep water channel, sliced through the sand by the powerful thrust of river and tide.

The fine clean sands of Exmouth have long been popular with bathers, but there are parts of the beaches where the shoreline currents are lethal and attention should be paid to the many warning notices covering specific areas. Orcombe Point and Rodney Point comprise the last high ground of the estuary. A customs watchhouse was established on Orcombe Point in 1740, to be replaced by a coastguard look-out which is now defunct. From the Point to Maer Rocks early sea defences were necessary to secure Exmouth's seaward expansion.

*Maer Rocks at the mouth of the Exe estuary. At low water they are ideal for anyone who likes exploring rock pools and catching crabs*

EXMOUTH IS DEVON'S oldest holiday resort. It escaped the impact of a rail link to Exeter until the mid-19th century and has less of the garishness of the big resorts to the west. The 2-mile (3.2km) promenade has an open and relaxed atmosphere and, above the seafront, fine Georgian houses on The Beacon add grace and elegance.

Exmouth has all the facilities of a good seaside town. The long expanse of beach offers all types of water sports although warning notices must be heeded. There is a heated swimming pool on the front and a sports centre in Imperial Road. Opposite Queen's car park on the seafront there is an impressive model railway exhibition.

Situated just outside the town, off the A376 in Summer Lane, is the remarkable 16-sided A La Ronde - the creation of 18th century cousins Jane and Mary Parminter. They built it as a combination of rustic cottage and neo-classic basilica based on San Vitale in Ravenna.

The building has a marvellously practical interior with rooms so placed as to trap the sun as the day progresses. Interior design includes feather friezes and a fascinating shell gallery in the cupola. It is open to visitors.

*Thatched, 16-sided A La Ronde — a charmingly eccentric house built on the northern edge of Exmouth by two ladies in 1795*

## ROUTE DIRECTIONS

**1**. Where the path branches along the estuary do not go straight on, but bear right and cross over a stile into a grassy play area. Turn left at the road, cross a bridge, then turn left to pass Danby House. Continue along a private road signposted Lower Halsdon Farm.

**2**. Go left over a stile and cross the railway line with care. Continue to the right along a concrete wall and down to the foreshore. From here walk along the sloping retaining wall. Regain the top of the wall and follow a vague path.

**3**. At a hedge, go right and round to the left with care, close to the railway track, then go over a stile into a field. Walk along the field, then cross a stile on to a narrow fenced-in path by the railway.

**4**. On reaching a road go left, then right and follow the lane into Lympstone.

THE RIVERSIDE VILLAGE of Lympstone is flanked by unexpected red cliffs which break the relative flatness of the estuary banks. The village has an equally unexpected nautical atmosphere with its narrow alley-ways running down to a tidal foreshore and harbour. Last century several dozen fishing boats used Lympstone harbour and vessels went as far as the Newfoundland Banks and Greenland.

The village has a fine mix of whitewashed thatched cottages and Regency villas. The latter were added when Lympstone attracted wealthy 19th century patrons seeking a heady mix of Devon air and the pungent aroma of river mud. The clock-tower on the foreshore was erected in 1885 by a northern merchant in memory of his wife's charitable work for the local poor.

For many years Lympstone was famous for its offshore oyster beds, the markers for which can still be seen at low tide. North of Lympstone is the Royal Marines training base of Lympstone Barracks. It lies close to Exton where most services are available.

The attractive village of Woodbury lies about 2 miles (3.2km) north-east of Lympstone. It has a fine village square and the church tower features some savage-looking gargoyles. To the east of the village is Woodbury Castle, an Iron Age earthworks.

*Lympstone, sliced right through by the railway line which hugs the estuary shore between Exmouth and Exeter, and its tiny harbour*

The link to Topsham from Lympstone can only be made by road walking or by public transport.

**1**. From Lympstone follow signs for Exeter to join the A376. Continue on the main road through Exton.

N

# TOPSHAM AND THE EXE ESTUARY

The River Exe is one of the West Country's great waterways; it rises on Exmoor and makes its way through Exeter to the sea. The estuary is wide and generous though without the depth of water or tidal regime that might have increased its industrial potential. This is perhaps no bad thing for aesthetic reasons.

Topsham (pronounced Tops'am if you do not wish to sound too much of a stranger) is the result of medieval politics. It benefited enormously from a territorial dispute in 1282 between the good citizens of Exeter and the Countess of Devon, Isabella de Fortibus. A dispute over Exeter's non-payment of a customary tithe of fish resulted in the Countess ordering a weir to be built across the river at the modern Countess Wear. Exeter fought for its rights in the courts and won its point in law though not in practice. It was not until the mid-16th century that the citizens obtained an Act of Parliament authorising a bypass canal which became the first inland waterway in England. The canal in its present form dates from last century.

Topsham flourished because of Countess Wear. It had always been a port closely connected with Exeter but after the building of the weir it became the city's main *entrepôt*, exporting minerals and cloth worldwide. Trading links with Holland and the resultant Dutch influence is reflected in the old merchants' houses, which were built of brick brought back from Holland by wool ships as ballast. Many of the houses on the Strand are converted warehouses, featuring the curved upper gables typical of Dutch vernacular architecture. The whole of the town is a

*Exmouth at the mouth of the estuary*

conservation area and a stroll through the narrow streets and alley-ways and along the waterfront is richly rewarding. A delightful museum occupies an old sail loft in a preserved `Dutch house' in Lower Shapter Street. The house is still owned by a distinguished local family, the Holmans, who have been ship-builders in Topsham for centuries. The town fits happily with the Exe estuary and a splendid bonus for the walker is that this is bird country writ large. The extensive mudflats and riverside meadows provide good feeding grounds for waders and wildfowl which congregate here in their thousands, and the estuary is also a major staging post for migratory birds.

*Topsham*

*The tidal River Exe at Topsham and the Exeter Ship Canal*

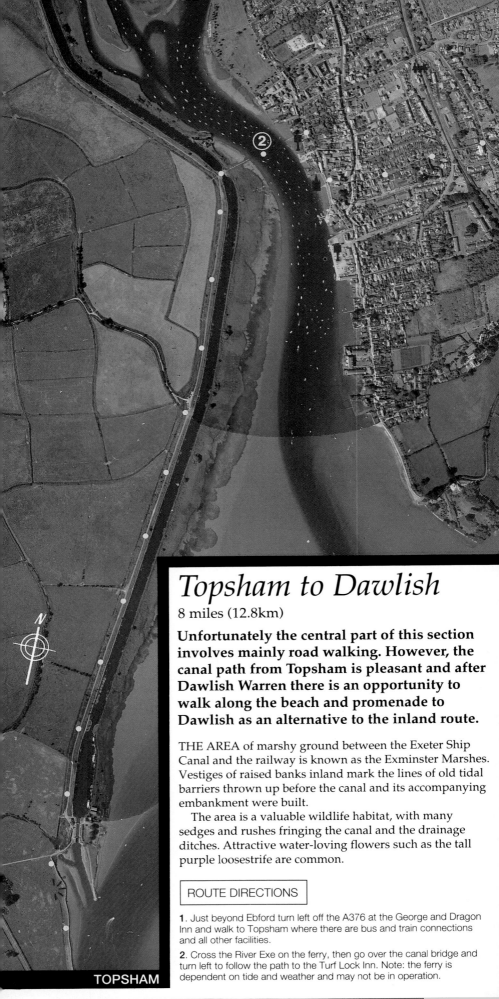

# Topsham to Dawlish

## 8 miles (12.8km)

**Unfortunately the central part of this section involves mainly road walking. However, the canal path from Topsham is pleasant and after Dawlish Warren there is an opportunity to walk along the beach and promenade to Dawlish as an alternative to the inland route.**

THE AREA of marshy ground between the Exeter Ship Canal and the railway is known as the Exminster Marshes. Vestiges of raised banks inland mark the lines of old tidal barriers thrown up before the canal and its accompanying embankment were built.

   The area is a valuable wildlife habitat, with many sedges and rushes fringing the canal and the drainage ditches. Attractive water-loving flowers such as the tall purple loosestrife are common.

### ROUTE DIRECTIONS

**1.** Just beyond Ebford turn left off the A376 at the George and Dragon Inn and walk to Topsham where there are bus and train connections and all other facilities.

**2.** Cross the River Exe on the ferry, then go over the canal bridge and turn left to follow the path to the Turf Lock Inn. Note: the ferry is dependent on tide and weather and may not be in operation.

TOPSHAM

THE TURF LOCK INN used to be the lockhouse and tollhouse at the tidal entrance to the Exeter Ship Canal. It has a fine setting and atmosphere and, like the canal itself, has remained in excellent condition. The lock gates are still intact.

The inn plays host to a large number of seasonal house martins which flit to and fro during the spring and summer months and feed on the myriad flies in the adjoining meadows. Opening hours at the inn are usually displayed on canal-side boards.

Powderham Castle, the official seat of the Earls of Devon, is open to the public during the summer season. The original castle was completed in the 1420s by Sir Philip Courtenay and the Courtenay family has lived there ever since. The modern building is the result of 18th and 19th century renovation after Civil War damage and is not particularly striking. Its sense of history is potent, however, given the Courtenay family's often dramatic involvement with courtly intrigue during the Elizabethan period. It is decorated and furnished in 18th and 19th century style and there are many fine portraits and paintings.

The surrounding park with its free-roaming deer is a special feature of Powderham, and the nearby church of St Clement, built of red breccia sandstone, is worth visiting.

*Powderham Castle and its extensive deer park lies sandwiched between the Exe estuary and the River Kenn*

## ROUTE DIRECTIONS

**1**. From the Turf Lock Inn follow the path alongside the embankment wall.

**2**. Cross the railway line with care as this is a very busy line. Turn left to join the road by Powderham church. For Powderham Castle, turn right. For Starcross, continue straight ahead.

POWDERHAM

STARCROSS SEEMS to be crammed against the estuary shoreline with road and railway squeezed between. It belongs to the estuary in many ways since it was originally an island site that was merged with the mainland as part of the massive embankment programme of the 1840s. The village has a famous sailing club that was founded in the 18th century and which is said to be the oldest in Britain. The ferry plies to and from Exmouth docks as it has done for centuries, and there are several nautical-sounding pubs in Starcross, plus the wonderful-sounding Atmospheric Railway Inn.

The inn is named after the village's famous relic of Isambard Kingdom Brunel's `atmospheric railway'. The Italianate building in weathered sandstone that stands between the modern railway and the main road was one of a number of pumping houses incorporated into this ingenious but ultimately impractical `silent' rail system.

The atmospheric railway connected Exeter and Teignmouth. Trains were driven by vacuum power contained within a continuous iron tube that ran between the rails. The iron tube had a slot along its entire length and was linked to the train by a piston and rod. A greased leather valve sealed the tube and opened and shut as the piston passed within. Air pressure behind the piston acted as an extra propellant.

Although the railway ran for some time, maintenance of the system proved to be a nightmare. Rats ate the grease with relish and chewed the leather, which also rotted due to chemical action. The pumps proved difficult to operate and the project was eventually abandoned at a loss of nearly £½ million. Steam locomotion soon became the norm and the Starcross pumping house is all that remains of one of Brunel's most ingenious inventions, and one which was environmentally sound in late 20th century terms.

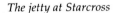

*N*

### ROUTE DIRECTIONS

**1**. There is no escape from road walking on this section. It is a case of best foot forward with a careful eye on the traffic travelling the A379 to Starcross.

**2**. From Starcross continue down the main road, then turn left on to the road through Cockwood. There is a pub and a shop here.

*The jetty at Starcross*

*Dawlish Warren nature reserve*

DAWLISH WARREN'S roadside attractions seem at odds with its magnificent wildlife reserve. The inland side of the railway offers numerous diversions for the holiday-maker, though much of the resort seems lifeless in the winter months. This is not so on its seaward sands. The barrier of the railway has helped to protect the huge sandspit reserve, which projects almost 1½ miles (2.4km) into the Exe estuary, from too much human intrusion. The name `Warren' dates from the 18th century when the dunes were used

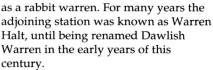

as a rabbit warren. For many years the adjoining station was known as Warren Halt, until being renamed Dawlish Warren in the early years of this century.

Most Coast Path walkers will be tempted to walk round the Warren, which is a major bird–roost and feeding site. Gannets, cormorants and shags are a common sight offshore, especially when large numbers of whitebait and sand eels go shimmering through the shallow waters. During the winter months, wildfowl, including wigeon, scoters, great crested grebes and the splendid great northern diver, are often present round the Warren.

The most significant bird area lies at the seaward end of the Warren on its northern side where large numbers of wading birds congregate, sometimes 20,000 at a time. There is a bird hide sited here from where species such as grey plovers, oyster-catchers, dunlin, godwits and several species of tern may be observed.

The plant life of the Warren is also fascinating because of its specialised environment. A tiny lilac-blue flower called the Warren crocus is unique to the area. Marsh orchids and the vivid evening primrose add to the delights, while round the saltmarshes sea aster and sea lavender flourish. In June a large area of tree lupin scrub at the Warren's eastern end provides a mass of brilliant yellow flowers.

### ROUTE DIRECTIONS

**1**. Continue along the road from Cockwood to reach the car park by the station at Dawlish Warren, which has refreshments and shops in plenty. The car park is down to the left of where the road bends sharply right by the Lee Cliff Park holiday apartments. Dawlish Warren nature reserve is reached by walking seaward through the narrow tunnel beneath the railway.

THE TOWN OF DAWLISH is focused on a central area known as The Lawn. This landscaped oasis with its trees and flower-beds, its small bridges and its fine bowling green, was formed in the early 19th century when the river known as The Brook was redirected. Fine houses with bow windows and iron lacework balconies were built on either side of the river and several still survive along The Strand and in Brunswick Place. The garden theme of Dawlish extends inland to Manor Grounds Park, and black swans and other waterfowl feed on the river. The surviving style of the Brunel railway station adds to Dawlish's sense of period charm. Jane Austen visited often and seemed to prefer Dawlish to Lyme Regis, and Charles Dickens also favoured the town as the birthplace of Nicholas Nickleby.

Dawlish has a fine museum specialising in Victoriana. It is reached by going up Brunswick Place alongside The Lawn then turning left to Barton Terrace. There is an indoor swimming pool in Playing Fields Road which can be reached by walking north from the station up Exeter Road.

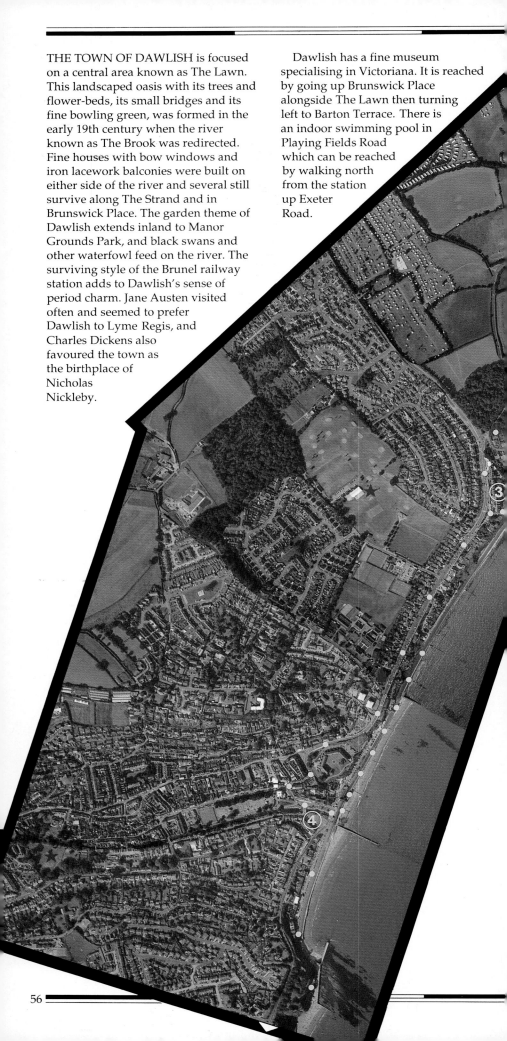

and a sign for St Mary's Church Hall. Go along a surfaced lane then on past the Langstone Cliff Hotel.

2. The path divides at a bench by some houses. The right branch leads quickly to the junction of Warren Road with the busy A379 Exeter road, from where a left turn leads to Dawlish. Alternatively, from the bench, continue on the direct path, passing a Great Western Railway boundary mark of 1918.

3. From above a landscaped area with benches it is possible to go down left and over a footbridge to link up with the sea-wall promenade to Dawlish. Otherwise continue a short distance along a surfaced path on to the A379 Exeter road, turning left for Dawlish.

## ROUTE DIRECTIONS

1. Dawlish can be reached from Dawlish Warren by walking along the beach or sea-wall promenade when tide and sea conditions permit. Otherwise, the official inland route starts just left of the sign for the Lee Cliff Park holiday apartments

4. From Dawlish station walk along Marine Parade. Continue up a steep walkway into Lea Mount Gardens. Go left past shelters and continue to an exit on to the Teignmouth road. Turn left, then veer left down a surfaced path on to Old Teignmouth Road.

*The beach at Dawlish, a mixture of sand and red shingle, with the railway alongside practically in the water*

# Dawlish to Maidencombe

6 miles (9.6km)

**Two contrasting stretches of the Coast Path make up this next section. Between Dawlish and Teignmouth there is a mixture of low-lying coastal and suburban terrain, but beyond the mouth of the Teign a more remote coastline offers some strenuous but enjoyable walking.**

THE CLIFF FEATURE known as the Parson and Clerk lies mid-way between Dawlish and Teignmouth. The distinctive mainland rock is the parson, and the offshore pinnacle is the clerk. They are said to represent a real-life pair who were out collecting tithes from reluctant tenants, got drunk on part of the proceeds, fell in with the Devil and finally fell in the sea and drowned. Now their sandstone effigies glare at each other on the Holcombe cliffs with mutual recriminations.

*Holcombe village behind the cliff formation known as the Parson and Clerk - at which point the railway temporarily disappears*

HOLCOMBE

---

ROUTE DIRECTIONS

**1.** Just past the junction with the main road turn left over a stile and down some wooden steps on to a path between post-and-wire fencing. Follow the path, which is steep in places, round field edges to Windward Lane. Go down to the main road and turn left.

**2.** Look out for the narrow entrance to Smugglers Lane on the left, opposite Hall Lane. Go down to the seafront, where there are toilets, then along a cobbled walkway under the railway arch to gain the sea-wall promenade. This is a low-tide, quiet-seas route. Access along the cobbled walkway may be blocked at high tides. If so, ignore Smugglers Lane and continue on the main Teignmouth Road to Cliff Road (opposite Oak Hill Cross Road). Turn down Cliff Road, then go right on to Cliff Walk which is followed to Teignmouth.

**3.** If sea conditions are favourable at the railway arch, walk along the sea-wall promenade.

ALTHOUGH A PLACE of subdued charm these days, Teignmouth has seen turbulent times - not least when it was sacked by the French navy in 1690. Like its many counterparts in South Devon, the town became a fashionable resort in the late 18th century. Today tourism is balanced by the working environment of the town's eastern riverfront, from where Dartmoor granite, timber and clay were exported and ball-clay is still shipped out in great quantity.

The resort has looked after its assets: its seafront and beaches attract holiday-makers and it is a popular windsurfing venue. The area behind the seafront known as the Den is nicely landscaped and there are some elegant Regency houses. Octagonal St James's Church off Bitton Park Road has a fine interior with striking cast-iron columns and a painted roof. The Teignmouth Museum in French Street is worth a stop, and a town regatta is held at the end of July.

Georgian Shaldon with its Regency villas and thatched cottages with flower-filled gardens matches Teignmouth for restrained charm. It is protected from the sea by the headland of The Ness through which a tunnel runs to the pleasant Ness Cove beach. The tunnel starts near the car park a short distance up from the Ness House Hotel. This feature is called the Smugglers Tunnel but was probably associated with lime burning and used as an access to the beach where coal vessels off-loaded.

The Shaldon Wildlife Collection, near the tunnel entrance, has chipmunks, monkeys, exotic birds and other small mammals.

---

ROUTE DIRECTIONS

**1**. Continue along the sea-wall promenade to reach Terrace Walk at Teignmouth. Walk along Teignmouth promenade.

**2**. Go past the small disused lighthouse at the end of the promenade, then bear right across the car park. Keep the lifeboat house on your left and go down to the ferry point on the beach.

**3**. On arrival at Shaldon go left along Marine Parade. Where the road curves inland, branch off left along a surfaced path in front of the Ness House Hotel.

**4**. Go up some steps on the right, then go left and steeply uphill into the trees. Follow the path round The Ness, then turn left on to a track beside a car park. Continue alongside a golf course.

LABRADOR BAY is a reminder of the trading links that ports such as Teignmouth had with Newfoundland and the Grand Banks cod fishery in the 18th century. Teignmouth played an important part in the Banks fishery through it boat-building industry and associated trades such as boot-making and tool-making, and many Teignmouth merchants of the period owned land in Newfoundland.

Most West Country fishing villages had connections with the Newfoundland fisheries, and in Devon there are as many Newfoundland Inns as there are Newfoundland Bays. The inns were well-known recruiting posts for the Grand Banks: many an adventurous youngster or unemployed man committed himself over too much strong drink to a sober life in the North Atlantic, with poor returns.

Devon boats worked the Grand Banks for several months at a time, salting the cod down and then taking the final catch to Portugal and Spain where Catholic fast days created a big demand for fish. Port would often be carried to England by the returning boats.

The coast south of Shaldon is particularly rich in wild flowers. Fertile soil, a sunny outlook and numerous belts of woodland and hedge encourage a host of plants. In spring and early summer the coastal walker has the bonus of such early `sunburst' flowers as primrose and lesser celandine, while the fruitful habitat between field and hedgerow produces the white flowers of blackthorn and cow parsley and the delicate blooms of greater stitchwort. Red campion and the smaller herb robert are abundant while the pinkish–red valerian appears a little later. The sweet-smelling, cream-coloured flowers of honeysuckle bloom towards the end of May. By June the more exotic-looking foxgloves and the `snow-drift' blossom of hawthorn crowd the borders of the path. Blackberries flower in June and are abundant along this stretch of coast during the autumn months when many flowering plants linger on and ivy adds its gloss to the hedgerows.

The east-facing estuary of the River Teign. A passenger ferry can be taken across the narrow strip of water at the mouth

ROUTE DIRECTIONS

**1**. Follow the path to the main road and turn left. After a few yards, keep left along a short-lived path that leads out on to a pavement bordering the road. Where the pavement ends go down steps leading left on to a footpath to Labrador Bay. (Pay attention to the notice and hang on to your clothes.)

**2**. Continue along the path via some steep sections.

*Shaldon, on the other side of the estuary. The wooded headland is called The Ness*

# Maidencombe to Torquay

7 miles (11km)

**The remote and peaceful first section of the Coast Path to Babbacombe soon merges with the suburban outskirts of Torquay where there is inevitably an increase in people due to the many car parks and access points to the coast. The Path makes the best of things by following the true coastline as often as possible.**

THE INACCESSIBLE STRETCH of coastline with its tiny coves south of Teignmouth was ideally suited to smuggling. On the coast of Labrador Bay there is a place called Smugglers' Hole, and numerous inland caches were sited at lonely farmhouses and inns where secret store-rooms were commonplace.

More respectable personalities also favoured this lovely stretch of the coast. Rudyard Kipling lived for a time at Maidencombe and Brunel planned his retirement estate inland of the Valley of the Rocks at Watcombe in a landscape safely out of sight and sound of hooting trains. Sadly, the great engineer died before the completion of the project.

## ROUTE DIRECTIONS

1. Follow the path between inland fields and thick scrub to where it joins a track by houses. Turn right and walk down to Maidencombe with its pub, refreshments during season, toilets and telephone.

2. Turn left into the car park. The Thatched Tavern is a few yards up the road. Walk across the car park, then turn left down the track towards the beach. Go past the toilets, then branch to the right over a stile and continue through woods.

3. Just past a bench-with-a-view, the path crosses a narrow section with an inside handrail. A stepped path then leads down into the deeply wooded glen of the Valley of the Rocks.

4. Reach the road above Watcombe Beach. Turn left, then immediately right. At a junction at the top of a slope keep straight ahead.

5. On reaching a T-junction beside a golf course, turn left.

*The undulating landscape behind Babbacombe Bay gives the coastline this delightful scalloped-edge effect*

MAIDENCOMBE

## ROUTE DIRECTIONS

**1**. Follow the path alongside the golf course, ignoring paths going off left until reaching an open park area with seats.

**2**. Go down left, then turn right to pass above a pagoda-style shelter and on to a narrow path. Continue steeply down a stepped path and then go over a rise to reach the cliff railway.

**3**. Go up right, then left under the railway incline. Turn down left, then bear right, then left again down stone steps to the road. Go down the road to a gate on a bend. Oddicombe Beach is to the left. In season, refreshments are available and there are toilets. Cross a metal stile beside the gate, then go down to a broad walkway above the sea. (A higher path leads from inside the gate past wooden benches and through the trees. This may be more convenient during stormy sea conditions.) Continue to Babbacombe where further sustenance can be obtained.

**4**. Walk up the steep road from Babbacombe harbour, then turn sharply left along a tarmac drive to climb some broad steps between houses. Follow the winding main path without diverting and reach a surfaced track. Go left, then more steeply left up a stepped path and into trees.

**5**. Continue on to the large open area of Walls Hill. The path stays close to the seaward fence all the way round to a break above the cliff-fringed Anstey's Cove. A path leads down via the break to the cove proper. The official Path continues alongside the fence, then down a path fringed with hawthorn trees. On reaching the road, turn left past the car park then turn left on to the main path round Black Head.

*A world in miniature at Babbacombe Model Village*

BABBACOMBE BAY is nicely protected from prevailing westerlies and Oddicombe Beach is pleasant, though popular. Babbacombe's cliff railway was built in 1926 and still operates during the season.

The famous Babbacombe Model Village is located in Hampton Avenue, St Marychurch. It can be reached by continuing up the side of the cliff railway to the upper station and on down Cliffside Road. The village is open all year and is more than the name implies. Laid out over 5 acres (2 hectares) of gardens linked by a working model railway, it replicates a complete slice of urban and rural England.

ANSTEY'S COVE became very popular with the Victorian sea-bathing fraternity and by the 1890s bathing machines lined the beach like bizarre Punch and Judy booths on wheels. Extremes in propriety reached a high point during this period. Bathing-machine owners had to supply ladies with voluminous costumes and towels while round the corner on supposedly 'isolated' beaches Victorian gents enjoyed nude bathing. The righteous were scandalised by 'forward women' who, 'not content with gazing from the cliffs . . . pass near the bathers . . .'

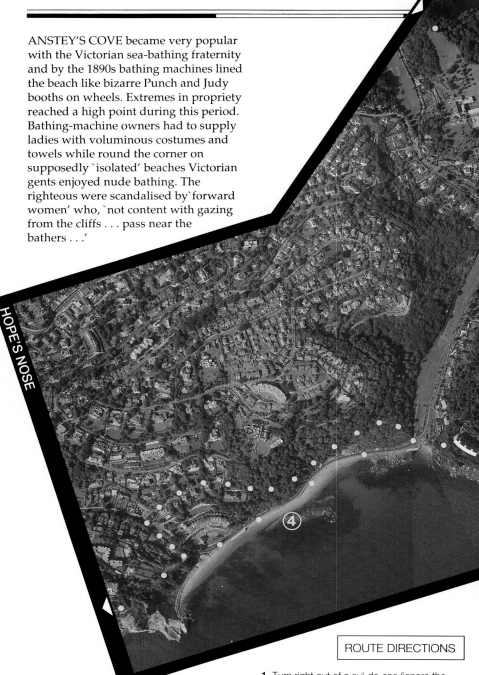

Kents Cavern lies just up from the point at which Anstey's Cove Road merges with Ilsham Road. This labyrinthine complex of tunnels and caves was lived in thousands of years ago at the same time that sabre-tooth tigers and mammoths flourished. The caverns have been extensively excavated by archaeologists and examination of the thousands of remains has provided a wealth of important information about the past. Storytellers bring this past to life during guided tours of the caves, which are open all year.

## ROUTE DIRECTIONS

**1**. Turn right out of a cul-de-sac (ignore the narrow path going left) to reach Ilsham Marine Drive. Cross the road,then turn left by a seat and follow a path that runs above Marine Drive. Where the path rejoins Marine Drive, cross the road to a signpost indicating a path to Hope's Nose. (This is an optional diversion since the same return has to be made to the road.)

**2**. From the Hope's Nose access point, walk down the road to the public open space of Hillway Close. Go down left, then walk round Thatcher Point.

**3**. Continue along the road until above Meadfoot Beach. Look out for a diversion down steps to the left into the car park.

**4**. Walk along the road from the car park, then turn left up a lane opposite the Osborne Hotel. (An alternative inland walk starts opposite the car park. Cross the road and go along the obvious path keeping left where it forks. Follow the path along by a wall. Do not go right where it is signposted to Lincombe Gardens. Instead, continue on to Hesketh Road. At the mainroad turn left, then cross over at the Osborne Hotel to continue up the lane as above.)

*The cliff railway saves a stiff climb up from Oddicombe Beach*

*The remains of Torre Abbey are preserved within the colourful municipal gardens behind Torre Abbey Sands*

TORRE ABBEY can be reached by following King's Drive from the far end of Torre Abbey Sands. A late 12th century foundation dedicated to St Norbert, the building was badly damaged at the time of the Dissolution of the Monasteries and was later converted into a private house. It was taken over by the Torquay Corporation earlier this century and now houses the Torbay Art Gallery and Museum. A monastic tithe barn contains Silvers Model World, an automated miniature display which includes a model circus.

## ROUTE DIRECTIONS

**1**. Continue up the lane, then go along a surfaced path with black posts at its entrance. Remain on the path and where it merges into a road (black-tipped posts) veer off left on a path up to Daddyhole Plain. Continue alongside the car park then go beneath an archway.

**2**. Follow a delightful path through Rock End Walk.

**3**. Where the path curves round below a house with handsome balustrades, continue straight ahead to reach the start of a road behind the Imperial Hotel. At the main road turn left and walk down to Torquay harbour.

**4**. Continue, keeping to the seaward side of the Torbay road.

# TORQUAY

Devon's most sophisticated resort began
modestly as a small hamlet and harbour
below Torre Abbey: it was known then
as Torre Key. The start of the French
wars in 1793 boosted the importance of
Tor Bay as a naval anchorage and `Tor
Quay' was used extensively by the
Channel Fleet. The equable climate and
lush surroundings of Tor Quay's hills
led naval officers and their families to
settle round the harbour; naval surgeons
considered the climate and atmosphere
to be health-giving and fashionable
society soon followed as the French
resorts became less salubrious
politically. Torquay's future was
assured; or its fate sealed, depending on
the point of view.

Modern Torquay owes much to
Victorian society which made it the
acme of seaside watering places and the
stylishness of Victorian architecture at
its best survives here, despite some late
20th century carelessness. There are
wide promenades and palm-fringed
parks and gardens, and exceptionally
fine Italianate villas of the early
19th century. Crescents and terraces of
elegant stucco houses - white-painted
and decorated with column, pediment
and pilaster - lie amid the wooded
hillsides of the Warberrys and
Lincombes. The Pavilion near Torquay
harbour was opened in 1912 and retains
an enduring neo-classicism, the whole
being enhanced with stylish copper
domes.

As Torquay expanded it absorbed the

*Wooded Black Head conceals Kents Cavern, a huge network of prehistoric caves and tunnels that has been turned into a major tourist attraction*

*During the summer ferries ply their way back and forth across the bay from the harbour at Torquay (seen above) to Brixham harbour*

adjoining villages of St Marychurch and Cockington. The latter has been faithfully preserved with its thatched cottages and 14th century forge still intact. It lies within a mile of Torquay harbour and horse-drawn landaus offer a pleasant trip to the village during the season. Alternatively, Cockington can be reached on foot from Corbyn Head along Seaway Lane.

There is much liveliness and bustle in Torquay during the summer and the town also remains healthily alive outside the holiday period. Most tastes are catered for with countless seaside attractions and there are many restaurants, pubs and clubs plus all main services. Attractions, apart from Torre Abbey, include Aqualand, the West Country's largest aquarium, situated on Beacon Quay where the Coast Path reaches Torquay harbour. Entertainment is available at theatres and cinemas while a harbourside leisure complex includes an indoor swimming pool.

# Torquay to Brixham
## 7 miles (11km)

The `Coast' Path between Torquay and Brixham is often dismissed too easily, consisting as it does of road walking through urban development. However, although the brazen shores of Torbay are certainly overcrowded at the height of the season, handsome promenades were built for promenading and for the reflective coastal walker there is interest in plenty with a number of pleasant off-road diversions. An alternative to this section during the season is to take the Western Lady ferry from Princess pier to Brixham (telephone the Torquay ferry office on Torquay 297292 for details).

PAIGNTON FALLS somewhere between Brixham and Torquay as far as character is concerned. Like its neighbours it was once a modest port, as the neat little harbour indicates, and the seafront can be a pleasure to walk along out of season. The town also has many attractions apart from the obvious ones of pier and beach.

The 14th century Kirkham House with its interesting exhibition of modern craftwork is reached by going directly inland from the pier to Mill Lane, off Cecil Road. Other attractions include the Festival Hall on the promenade, an aquarium on the harbourside, and the famous Paignton Zoo at the junction of Totnes Road and Penwill Way.

*Paignton Pier lies midway betweeen the harbour and Redcliffe, the headland separating the two beaches*

*The sweep of Torbay, almost solidly built-up along its entire length*

| ROUTE DIRECTIONS |
| --- |

**1**. Continue past Livermead Head, looking out for the huge gas tank on the opposite side of the road. Go left through gates into Hollicombe Gardens, previously the municipal gasworks and now delightfully transformed. Walk across the gardens to the far right corner, then go left across the railway and turn right through a grassed area to reach the seafront. (If the gardens are shut, walk a short distance along the main road and take the first turning left, then cross the railway.)

**2**. Continue along the seafront then, at a hotel, detour right on to the main road, then go back left. Walk along Paignton promenade to the pier.

TORBAY

AT GOODRINGTON the overtly urban nature of Torbay changes. The village has much green space around it and is protected from too much seaside development by handsome Roundham Gardens to the north and by a gradual merging into countryside to the south. The resort is popular, however, and has a fine beach with safe bathing and many rock pools.

From Goodrington the walkers' route runs alongside the Paignton and Dartmouth Railway which operates steam trains to Kingswear; its carriages bear the distinctive chocolate and cream livery of the Great Western Railway. The line was closed by British Rail in 1972, but was soon taken over by the Dart Valley Railway Company who re-opened it in 1973 using GWR stock, adding to its lustre by running the famous *Flying Scotsman*. The steam locomotives are beautifully maintained and make a nostalgic sight.

Walkers with a taste for indoor swimming could make their way to the Torbay leisure centre and swimming pool situated a short distance inland from Goodrington Beach. It can be reached by walking up Tanner's Road to cross the main Dartmouth road.

*Goodrington Sands, on the southern side of Roundham Head, attracts sun-bathers in their thousands as it is so easily accessible*

ROUTE DIRECTIONS

**1.** From Paignton harbour go up Roundham Road and turn left into Cliff Road. Walk through the pleasant Roundham Gardens, then bear down left along a twisting surfaced walkway to the seafront at Goodrington. There are bus and rail connections here as well as the usual facilities.

**2.** Walk all the way along Goodrington seafront to where the promenade road ends at toilets. Go down steps and walk under the railway bridge. Turn left immediately up steps and follow a surfaced walkway alongside the railway.

**3.** Follow the path across Sugar Loaf Hill, keeping the railway on your left. Ignore a surfaced track leading under a railway bridge.

GOODRINGTON SANDS

## ROUTE DIRECTIONS

**1**. Cross a field. Take the left-hand path up some steps, then down other steps to the road. Turn left and go under a bridge to reach Broad Sands beach and promenade. There are refreshments, toilets and telephones here.

**2**. From the end of the promenade at Broad Sands follow the path round the edge of the cliff and alongside a golf course. Keep to the left-hand path after Churston Point, then go down to Elberry Cove.

**3**. Walk along the beach, then go up some steps into a wood. Continue steeply, and where the path forks keep left. Continue through woods and on down to the pebbly beach at Churston Cove.

**4**. From Churston Cove follow the path across rocks (ignore sign indicating inland path), then go up through the trees and through a kissing-gate. Go down a narrow path and along the road. Just past the turning to Fishcombe Cove turn left through a gap in the wall on to a surfaced path, which leads down steps to the Freshwater Quarry car park.

*Top right:*
*Walkers need to be on the alert as they pass the dramatically sited golf course above Elberry Cove*

THIS SOUTHERN CORNER of Torbay enjoys the double blessing of an eastern outlook and protection from prevailing westerlies. The cliffs, rarely punished by salt-laden winds, are covered with wild flowers in spring and summer. On Sugar Loaf Hill primroses are particularly abundant in the spring.

Overall there is a mood of peace, yet twice in its history this quiet corner has witnessed military activity of major proportions. During the Second World War the beaches and low cliffs around Broad Sands and Elberry Cove were used for mock-landing exercises by thousands of American troops. These were linked to similar though much larger and more dramatic exercises further south at Slapton and Torcross. The exercises were intended to familiarise the troops with conditions expected at the Normandy landings.

More than 250 years before that time, European troops had come ashore at Churston Cove when William of Orange landed at Brixham during the bloodless revolution of 1688. The event heralded the end of Stuart and Catholic influence in Britain and secured the country for the Protestant cause. William came with 670 ships and as Brixham could not cope with the influx of 30,000 men, Churston Cove served as the disembarkation point.

# Brixham to Dartmouth

10 miles (16km)

*N*

**This is one of the most strenuous sections of the Coast Path and provides a brisk and rewarding antidote to the easy stroll along Torbay. There are no convenient refreshment points after Berry Head, but this is more than compensated for on arrival at Dartmouth.**

BRIXHAM IS A bustling place with a large fleet of trawlers and smaller boats, a busy fish market and a well-placed marina. A replica of the *Golden Hind* is moored in the harbour and is open to the public. Close by is the British Fisheries Museum in the Old Market House, while the Marine Aquarium and Trawling Exhibition on the quay is also worth visiting. Brixham Museum and the National Coastguard Museum is at Bolton Cross, along Fore Street. The 200ft-high (60m) cliffs of Berry Head are an important bird sanctuary and the Head has been designated a nature reserve and country park.

## ROUTE DIRECTIONS

1. Walk round Brixham harbour past the yacht marina and breakwater. Continue across a pebble beach and go up steps, turning left along Berry Head Road.

2. Enter Berry Head country park and follow signs out to the main battery.

3. Walk to the Southern Fort. Skirt the fort on its landward side. Continue past a chalet park at Durl Head and bungalows above St Mary's Sands.

4. Go down concrete steps then turn right up steps and along a passage way, then turn left. Continue down a stepped path through trees, turn right at a track then go left through a gate and continue round Sharkham Point.

5. Beyond Sharkham Point climb steeply to Southdown Cliff.

*Berry Head country park on the headland jutting out beyond Brixham*

THE COAST SOUTH of Sharkham Point is highly complex geologically with Meadfoot slates and Staddon grits alternating as far as Scabbacombe. The manner in which they have eroded has given rise to the rather sharp-edged roller-coaster country. Certainly, the walker feels that he is going against the grain of the country along an unrelenting switchback of high points and sea-level combes, with descents often pitched at awkward angles. In wet weather care is needed on some of the muddier slopes. All this makes for challenging and enjoyable walking although the honest pattern of ups and downs - a biting climb followed by an airy stroll on the cliff tops - that is found on the Sidmouth coast is missing. The old lime kiln at Man Sands used

limestone from Berry Head while coal would have been landed on the beach from Welsh collier vessels.

## ROUTE DIRECTIONS

**1.** Descend steeply to Man Sands and cross the beach past an old lime kiln. Follow the track going right, then up left, then go to the right over a stile into the National Trust's Woodhuish property.

**2.** Walk up the field and go over a stile or through a gate into a field. Follow the path leading directly ahead and up the steep slope, between patches of scrub.

**3.** Continue along the edge of fields, then descend very steeply to a dip. Go up and over a small hill keeping to seaward to reach a plank bridge above Scabbacombe Sands.

**4.** From above Scabbacombe Beach climb a steep, stepped path, then continue round the seaward face of the head to Downend Point.

*Urban development is left behind as the Coast Path continues over the haphazard rock formations of Southdown Cliff*

SOUTHDOWN CLIFF

THE HOUSE AND GARDENS of Coleton Fishacre are the creation of the D'Oyly Carte family. The site was bought in 1925 by Rupert D'Oyly Carte, the son of Richard D'Oyly Carte who staged Gilbert and Sullivan operas, and Lady Dorothy planted 18 acres with rare and exotic plants between the mid-1920s and 1940. The garden is open to the public at advertised times.

**4.** Climb some railed-in concrete steps then turn left up an old shell-ramp and past concrete bunkers. Continue up concrete and brick steps to an open grassy area behind an old building. Follow the path down left, keeping left at a junction.

## ROUTE DIRECTIONS

**1.** The path zig-zags steeply up the face of the Point to a T-junction. Go left and continue with some tough up and down walking through impressively ragged scenery to descend into the green depths of Pudcombe Cove.

**2.** Cross a small bridge and turn left. (The path to the right gives access to the National Trust's Coleton Fishacre Garden.) Above Pudcombe Cove Beach, with its old swimming pool, go right and uphill. Continue round Outer Froward Point to reach a T-junction. Turn left and cross a stile on to a broad track running through an area of felled trees.

**3.** A short distance along the rough track veer down left on to a path. (Continuing along the rough track offers a short-cut to the top of Inner Froward Point.) Continue through trees, then down to a T-junction with a railed path that leads round the Point.

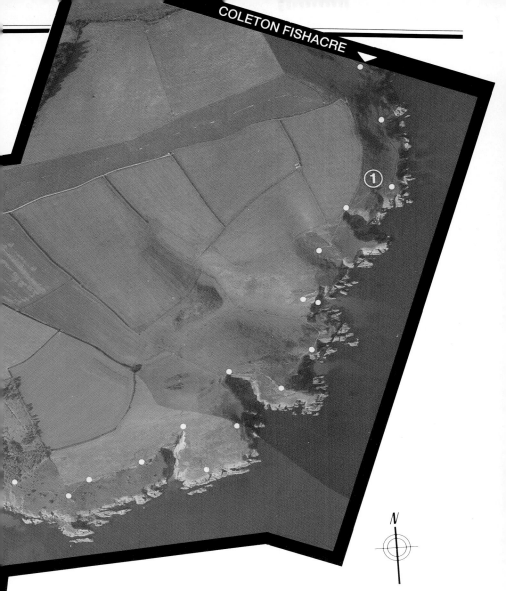

*Above the deep plunge of Pudcombe Cove lies Coleton Fishacre Garden*

## ROUTE DIRECTIONS

**1.** Descend steeply to Mill Bay Cove and turn right by an old mill with a fine turret. Go left and up through woods to some solid wooden steps leading on to a private road. Go left past some houses and round behind Brookhill Flats.

**2.** Where the road branches just past a house, bear down left, then left again. Look out for steps leading down left just before the end of Beacon Road. Go down the steps, then turn right under an archway to the top of the ferry slip at Kingswear. The vehicle ferry takes passengers to the slipway closest to Dartmouth Castle. The passenger-only ferry lands at Dartmouth's main quay a short distance to the north.

**3.** From the vehicle ferry landing slip on the Dartmouth side, take the first left on to the cobbled quay at Bayard's Cove. Go through the old fort at the end of the quay and through a gun port. Climb the steps, then turn left. Follow the road and branch left down Castle Road. Keep to the path alongside the lower road to the castle car park.

**4.** From the seaward end of the castle car park take the path going up to the right through woods to reach a road. Follow the path which leads off the road. Ignore the surfaced track on the left. Where the path forks go right and reach the road just before Compass Cottage. Go left, then turn left off the road towards the sea.

# DARTMOUTH AND KINGSWEAR

The Dart is the loveliest and most romantic of Devon's rivers and its narrow entry to the sea is fittingly dramatic. Yet the river is wide enough to accord space and elegance to Dartmouth when viewed from the east bank. Good Devon buildings rise in tiers from the long quayside to the commanding façade of the Dartmouth Naval College, with a swell of green fields beyond.

Kingswear has seen more modest times than its neighbour while being linked irrevocably to its turbulent

history. The village is noted for its shellfish boats and is a prestigious yachting centre with a fine marina. It is also the southern terminus of the Paignton and Dartmouth Steam Railway.

Military conflict and naval connections have been key elements in Dartmouth's history. The Romans occupied the port; the town was burnt by the French in the 12th century; it was unsuccessfully invaded by the French in 1404, and later burnt again by the same old enemy. Dartmouth became embroiled in the 17th-century Civil War on the side of Parliament, fell to the Royalists under Prince Rupert and was recaptured by Fairfax. Relative peace

33,000 American troops left Dartmouth for the D-Day landings. Even the Pilgrim Fathers managed a quick unscheduled call for repairs.

The port's turbulent past is marked by surviving fortifications on both banks of the river mouth. Kingswear Castle is now a private residence while Dartmouth Castle has survived intact and is open to the public. Both castles were built in the late 15th century. During emergencies a heavy chain was raised between the two as an effective barrier across the mouth of the river. A 20th century gun battery remains intact on Inner Froward Point and is threaded by the Coast Path.

*Dartmouth's castle at the harbour entrance*

*The Britannia Royal Naval College*

*Dartmouth and Kingswear on either side of the estuary*

reigned until the town was heavily bombed during the Second World War.

Throughout all this Dartmouth remained at the heart of English maritime life. In the 12th century Richard I set out on his Crusade from Dartmouth with 100 ships; the town sent 31 ships to the siege of Calais in 1346, and in 1944, 485 ships carrying

Dartmouth has some fine architecture. There is a terrace of 17th century houses and a restored customs house on Bayard's Quay. The 17th century Butter walk in Duke Street was beautifully restored after 1940s bomb damage. Dartmouth's maritime museum with its wealth of maritime artefacts and memorabilia contained within panelled rooms is also in Duke Street, while the town's oldest building, The Cherub, with its famous bar and restaurant, is in Higher Street. The 18th century Manor House in St George's Square, off Fairfax Place, has some fine baroque plasterwork. It is open to the public. In Mayor's Avenue is the Newcomen Engine House. Thomas Newcomen was a Dartmouth man and his seminal influence on early steam engine technology is celebrated here.

Dartmouth also has several splendid pubs and restaurants, all main services and good shopping facilities.

# Dartmouth to Torcross

9 miles (14.4km)

**The Coast Path is not continuous from Dartmouth Castle to Strete Gate. Unpleasant road walking is one option, but there is an alternative route which follows a tortuous but very enjoyable series of inland diversions that keep the walker off roads for most of the way. From Strete Gate a direct path alongside Slapton Ley is then followed.**

GALLANTS BOWER, above Dartmouth Castle, is a delightfully wooded hill crowned with the remnants of an earthwork which was built by Royalist forces during the Civil War. There are fine views to Inner Froward Point on the eastern shore. The distinctive 80ft-high (24m) daymark tower situated inland from Froward Point was built in 1864 as a navigational aid for Royal Mail vessels seeking the entrance to the Dart.

The Coast Path along the top of Little

Dartmouth Cliffs is a relatively recent introduction. There was no access until the 1970s when the property was purchased with funds raised through a local appeal and from the National Trust's Enterprise Neptune Fund. A notable contribution came from the Devon Federation of Women's Institutes in commemoration of its golden jubilee.

*Combe Point and Dancing Beggars, land owned by the National Trust*

## ROUTE DIRECTIONS

**1.** Continue round Blackstone Point then cross a bridge over a sea-washed ravine. Go uphill and cross a stile, then climb steeply to a bench where the path turns left.

*2.* Follow the path through a gate and past an old telegraph cable sign and continue to where the path goes through a gap in a wall, then bear right. Above Warren Cove bear right, then go through a gate and continue inland to the National Trust car park at Redlap.

**3.** Turn left out of the car park and follow the narrow lane that winds down to meet the main A379 outside Stoke Fleming. Here shops, a telephone and bus connections can be found.

DURING THE 13th century Stoke Fleming was in the ownership of the Le Fleming family. Its unspoilt church of St Peter, which has some fine brasses, dates from that period.

In the valley running down to Blackpool Sands a fierce battle was fought in 1404 between French invaders with their eyes on Dartmouth, and local militia who repulsed them. Blackpool Sands is popular in the summer but is still worth a visit for its fine sands and good swimming.

ROUTE DIRECTIONS

Strete Gate can be reached from Stoke Fleming by walking directly south along the A379 for just over 3 miles (4.8km). It makes for unpleasant walking, however. The following alternative runs inland via pleasant back roads and green lanes. It demands concentration on route-finding.

**1.** Turn left at the A379, then cross the road with care to the entrance of Ravensbourne Lane. Go through a narrow gate on the right into a sports field. Walk down the left side of the field to emerge at the junction of Ravensbourne Lane and Venn Lane. Turn right and after a few yards cross left and go through a gate. Turn left down a

*Blackpool Sands*

narrow, surfaced path between wire fencing to emerge into Rectory Lane with Stoke Fleming church directly ahead.

**2.** Turn right out of Rectory Lane and walk up the road. Where it bends round to the right, take the road branching left. This becomes a rough track which then turns down right and becomes a narrow rocky path which is often wet. Where the path joins a road, turn left.

**3.** Turn right at thatched cottages on to the main road above Blackpool Sands (refreshments, toilets, telephone). Cross a bridge, then go right up a lane for a short distance. Turn left into a green lane.

**4.** Follow the lane to where it becomes surfaced just past a house. Continue to a T-junction. Turn right and follow the road round left past old curved barns at Landcombe.

*Stoke Fleming lies along the A379 which winds down behind Blackpool Sands*

②

③

④

P

THE LAST SECTION of path leading down to Strete Gate is part of the old road, or `strete', that ran from Dartmouth towards Plymouth. A gate and fence was erected at Strete Gate in the distant past for controlling the cattle which grazed on the grass of the shingle ridge. A manor house built at Strete Gate in the 1870s became a hotel in 1937, was requisitioned by the military in 1943, and later fell into ruin. The car park marks the site.

## ROUTE DIRECTIONS

**1.** Just past the curved barns, turn off right in front of some houses and follow a surfaced lane running parallel but counter to the main road. Follow the lane as it curves round to the left, then go sharply right alongside the gable-end of a house and down a green lane. Follow a narrower path across a housing estate road, then another road to reach a third road.

**2.** Turn left, then right into Hynetown Road just above the church of St Michael at Strete. The village has a pub, a shop, a telephone and a youth hostel. Follow the road round several bends to the A379.

**3.** Turn right down the A379 for a short distance then, just beyond a lay-by on the left, turn left on to a surfaced path. Continue to Strete Gate.

**4.** Cross the main road from the end of the access lane to Strete Gate car park, then turn left down the path alongside the Ley.

*The village of Strete behind the stretch of sand at Pilchard Cove*

SLAPTON SANDS

*Slapton Ley, separated from the sea by a shingle ridge, is designated a Site of Special Scientific Interest*

THE GREAT STRETCH of Slapton Ley is the largest freshwater lake in the South West. Covering an area of 445 acres (180 hectares), the Ley was formed after the end of the last Ice Age about 10,000 years ago. Rising sea-levels pushed up a bank of eroded quartz and flint shingle to form the present barrier, then rivers and streams flowed into the depression.

Slapton Ley is a major nature reserve with remarkable reed bed and freshwater habitats. It is owned by the Herbert Whitley Trust and is managed by the Slapton Ley Field Centre which is based at Slapton village. The Centre publishes a number of information booklets and there is a waymarked trail through part of the reserve, starting from the boathouse beyond Slapton Bridge.

Slapton village has a rare pedigree though it suffered badly when it was taken over for six months during the last war when extensive D-Day exercises involved thousands of mainly American troops (note the memorial on Slapton Beach). The village was evacuated and several buildings, including the church, were damaged by shell fire.

Slapton was owned initially by Sir Guy de Brien, one of those remarkable 14th-century grandees who combined military valour with great urbanity. De Brien founded the chantry college of St Mary at Slapton, of which the rather baleful but striking ruined tower remains. The village has good pubs and there are shops and a post office.

---

ROUTE DIRECTIONS

**1.** Keep to the path between the road and the Ley. The side road at Slapton Bridge is crossed midway.

# Torcross to Salcombe

12 miles (19.2km)

**The Coast Path to Salcombe goes through a delightful and dramatic area of rugged headlands and lonely coves. There are no refreshment facilities beyond Beesands, without diverting inland.**

THE TRADITIONAL FISHING villages of Torcross and Beesands took a battering from the sea as recently as the late 1970s, when massive storms breached their defences. New sea walls and boulder ridges have since been erected.

Both places have refreshingly open aspects and are excellent watersports centres when the sea is in a passive mood.

A visit to the desolate remains of Hallsands village is salutory. The thriving fishing village of over 40 houses was lost to the sea because of massive dredging of shingle from Start Bay at the turn of the century.

*Torcross at the end of Slapton Ley*

ROUTE DIRECTIONS

**1.** Continue alongside the Ley to the car park at Torcross. Here there are shops, refreshments, toilets and bus connections. Cross the road from the car park and go on to the seafront walkway.

**2.** Go up steps at the end of the promenade. Follow a passageway to where it opens out behind some houses, then continue to a lane. Turn left, then veer up right past a private garage to bear left along a surfaced path and into a field.

**3.** Continue straight to pass through a gate which is signposted Circular Walk. Follow the path above a wooded quarry and continue down to reach Beesands Beach. Turn right and walk to Beesands village.

**4.** Go through the village to its end, then go up right in front of a thatched cottage and follow the path across Tinsey Head.

**5.** Walk across the beach at North Hall sands. Bear sharp right below the hotel, then left again and up wooden steps to reach Trouts holiday flats above old Hallsands village. A path leads down left to the remains of the village.

*All that is left of Hallsands on the rocky ledge below the cliff*

TORCROSS

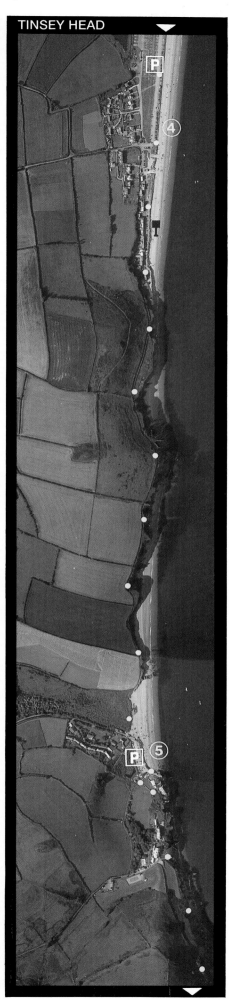

TINSEY HEAD

THE NAME START comes from the Saxon word for tail, a fitting description for this stormy promontory of ragged slate. Start was reputedly a gallows site in medieval times where local pirates were hung in chains as a deterrent to their rascally companions.

Neolithic settlers colonised the cliff slopes around Start and gathered flint pebbles from the beaches at Peartree Cove to the south-west. At the adjoining Great Mattiscombe Sand there are dramatically eroded sea stacks crowned with vegetation.

Start Point and its western neighbour Prawle Point proved lethal to shipping for centuries. The great `tail' of the headland continues beneath the sea to the south-east as the Skerries Bank and this, coupled with a vicious tidal race, made the area so dangerous that a lighthouse was established in 1836. Even then the headland and its turbulent seas claimed many victims, with five vessels being lost during one storm in March 1891. The lighthouse is currently open to visitors at certain times during the summer.

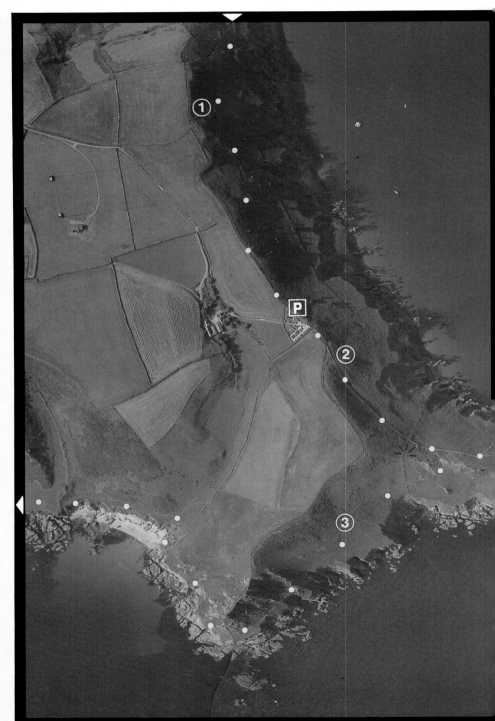

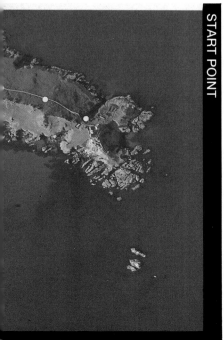

START POINT

*Start Point, spreading into the sea like the tail of a great sea monster*

## ROUTE DIRECTIONS

**1.** Follow the path steadily uphill to reach a car park above Start Point.

**2.** Go down the surfaced road towards the lighthouse. Break off right just past a wooden shack and cross the shoulder of the headland. (There is no official linking path round the headland via the lighthouse.)

**3.** Continue along the rocky path above the dramatic shoreline and below narrow ridges that rise inland.

LANNACOMBE IS A pleasant little cove with a small beach. It is linked by road to the A379 and there is a small car park above the beach. The cove was a well-known smuggling base. Local people would help land goods, such as brandy, tea, tobacco, spices and silk, from Torbay fishing smacks. Records show that large numbers of horses, each with an armed rider, would carry contraband swiftly out of combes such as Lannacombe and thence along a network of safe houses, barns and caches in the Devon countryside.

Smuggling was a bloody business at times as the Preventive Service sought to curb it from a base at Salcombe. Customs men were badly beaten and government revenue cutters often exchanged fire with heavily armed smuggling vessels. There was complicity however and pay-offs made to some Preventive officers. This gave rise to the contemporary phrase `bank-note blinkers'.

There are the remains of an old mill at Lannacombe and millstones lie beside the Coast Path.

(1)

*In summer the narrow road through the combe to popular Lannacombe Beach becomes congested and parking at the bottom is limited*

## ROUTE DIRECTIONS

**1.** Continue along a narrow rocky section of path below King's Head Rock, taking care when close to the cliff edge. Sheep are grazed in this area and dogs are best kept on a lead.

**2.** Cross above the beach at Lannacombe and pass a house and the site of an old mill. Bear left along the track and at the gate to a private house keep to the left of a post-and-rail fence.

**3.** At Woodcombe Sand follow a track that passes behind a tree-shrouded house. Just before the point where the track bends inland, go left down a vegetated path and cross a small stream. Turn left on to a rocky path along the base of the towering Woodcombe Point. Continue to Maelcombe Point.

The coastguard station on Prawle Point, another piece of the coast in the care of the National Trust

A SEQUENCE OF wave-cut platforms with inland `sea-cliffs' lies to the east of Prawle Point. These phenomena were caused by fluctuations in sea-level during the Ice Age. The fields along the shoreline lie on top of the eroded debris left after the Ice Age.

Named from the Old English for look-out, or the more colloquial peep, Prawle Point has been a look-out and signal station for centuries. The headland is ruggedly impressive with a distinctive archway on its seaward edge. Its strategic position as Devon's most southerly point explains the bunkers to the east; they date from the Second World War.

ROUTE DIRECTIONS

**1.** Follow the path along the seaward edge of fields. At one point it bends very sharply round to the left, then curves back to the right along the bottom edge of a field. Continue round Langerstone Point.

**2.** Continue along the coastal shelf past distinctive inland cliffs.

**3.** Pass an old war bunker. East Prawle with its shop, pub, toilets and bus connections, lies just under a mile inland. Go uphill in front of a row of houses then cross the shoulder of Prawle Point by keeping close to the right-hand hedge.

**4.** Continue above the attractive Maceley Cove which can be reached, with care, down a steep path. Cross the neck of the magnificent Gammon Head.

ALTHOUGH THE porcine names along this section of the South Devon coast are entertaining, there seems to be no real rhyme or reason to them. Many landmark names, such as Gammon Head, Ham Stone, Hamstone Cove and Pig's Nose, may relate to the fancied shapes of the rock features. Gammon Head especially has the proportions of a fine leg of ham and may have led to the other names. However, such names often originate from a defunct language and become conveniently corrupted into our own. This area of South Devon is known as the South Hams, a name derived from a Saxon word for shelter and may be connected with the 'ham' theme of the coastal features, although there is precious little shelter along here except for the eastern side of Gammon Head. Rather inappropriately, Bullock's Cove appears at the tail-end of the porcine trail.

The well-placed Gara Rock Hotel was built as a line of coastguard houses in the days when local people operated the service. Much of the Coast Path network follows old coastguard patrol routes,

and the Salcombe area was particularly advantageously placed for look-out points. The whitewashed look-out (below the Gara Rock hotel) with its conical thatched roof is a charming survival from those days.

There are very few fully manned coastguard look-outs round the south–west coast these days as sophisticated radio technology has taken over from manned 'watches'. Valuable local knowledge is retained, however, through the auxiliary coastguard service.

### ROUTE DIRECTIONS

**1.** Keep to the lower path along the cliff edge.
**2.** At Little Seacombe Sand bear right on an uphill track to pass directly below the garden wall of the Gara Rock Hotel. Follow the path round and down to the left below the thatched look-out. (An alternative route from Little Seacombe Sand leads directly ahead from the start of the uphill track. This path leads up steeply through deep bracken to join the main path just below the look-out.)
**3.** Follow the path along the edge of the cliffs and through rock outcrops to Portlemouth Down.

*Kingsbridge at the end of its estuary inland from Salcombe*

PORTLEMOUTH DOWN

IN MEDIEVAL TIMES East
Portlemouth was of greater importance
than Salcombe. Trade with other ports
increased its prosperity and the area's
European connections are reflected in
the church of St Winwaloe, or Guenole,
a 6th century Breton missionary who is
also associated with Landewednack on
the Lizard Peninsula.

## ROUTE DIRECTIONS

**1.** Follow the path round Rickham Common, then
through delightfully shady woods to reach the
sandy beach at Mill Bay.

**2.** Follow the surfaced road to the ferry at East
Portlemouth and cross to Salcombe. (There is a
ferry service from Salcombe to South Sands
which cuts out some road walking.)

**3.** Go up the ferry steps, then turn left along Fore
Street (the harbour is down to the right). Take the
left branch, signposted Sharpitor, and follow the
road steeply downhill to North Sands where a
dog-leg corner leads steeply up and left and then
down to South Sands with its refreshments and
toilets.

**4.** Continue up the road behind the hotel at South
Sands, then go left and along the road signposted
Sharpitor/Bolt Head.

**5.** Go through the entrance to the National Trust's
Overbecks Museum and Gardens, then bear left
at a junction on to the Courtenay Walk. The lane
up to the right leads to Overbecks.

# SALCOMBE

A yachting centre of great self-esteem, this beautifully situated resort thrives on the custom of boating enthusiasts and visiting yacht crews. Lying a mile inland from the open sea on the Kingsbridge estuary, its sheltered anchorage has made it one of the largest yachting centres in England. High winds make for high prices, however, and Salcombe is an unashamedly up-market place of some sophistication - but one with a gloriously rough and rousing past.

The Kingsbridge estuary is a drowned river valley. Enclosed by wooded hills, it has a serene climate and although a secure haven its notorious sandbar still poses a navigational hazard. The bar claimed the lives of 13 out of 15 lifeboatmen in 1916 when the Salcombe lifeboat was overwhelmed while returning from a cancelled mission.

The estuary, which is fed by five creeks and runs for nearly 5 miles (8km) inland, has been used by all manner of shipping for hundreds of years, and became notorious throughout the 16th and 17th centuries as the resort of pirates, smugglers and the general run of entrepreneur who trod a thin line between crime and enterprise on the high seas.

Boat-building was a major industry at Salcombe although East Portlemouth, from where the walker takes a short-lived but delightful ferry trip, was the centre of ship-building in medieval times, with the surrounding oak woods supplying the timber. The mid-18th century saw the high-point of the trade,

with hundreds of wooden ships being built by a thriving community of craftsmen. Salcombe clippers sailed world-wide from the port and brought home exotic prizes. Local fishermen were also noted for their skills, especially catching shellfish, and Salcombe still has several `crabbers'.

Shipping money built many of Salcombe's handsome villas such as those in elegant Devon Road and modern up-country affluence has transformed the old boat-building and

*Salcombe, with the tiny village at*
*East Portlemouth on the opposite bank*

fishing quarters into fashionable residences. The town is a lively and attractive place in season with its busy harbour front and its narrow streets such as Fore Street, Folly Lane and Robinson's Row. There are several pubs and restaurants where fine sea food is a speciality. The Museum of Maritime and Local History is in Cook's Boat Store on The Quay.

③

# Salcombe to Bigbury-on-Sea

11 miles (17.6km)

**An exhilarating walk along the lofty heights of Bolt from `Head' to `Tail', through some of the most spectacular cliff scenery on the South Devon coast. The River Avon poses a challenge if the seasonal ferry is not running, but a way round is available if wading deters the walker.**

THE NATIONAL TRUST property at Sharpitor, Overbecks, houses a youth hostel and museum and is surrounded by a fascinating garden. The museum was the creation of Otto Overbeck, a Dutch chemist and inveterate collector. It includes shipping exhibits, agricultural implements and a fine collection of British moths and butterflies.

ROUTE DIRECTIONS

**1.** Follow the narrow and stony path round the seaward nose of Sharp Tor and below its startling pinnacles. Go downhill to above Starehole Bay and up the steeper slope to the summit of Bolt Head.

**2.** Cross the rocky shoulder of Bolt Head and continue along the cliff edge.

**3.** Follow the path alongside clifftop fields.

*Precariously placed properties above Stink Cove - a place strikingly at odds with its unattractive name*

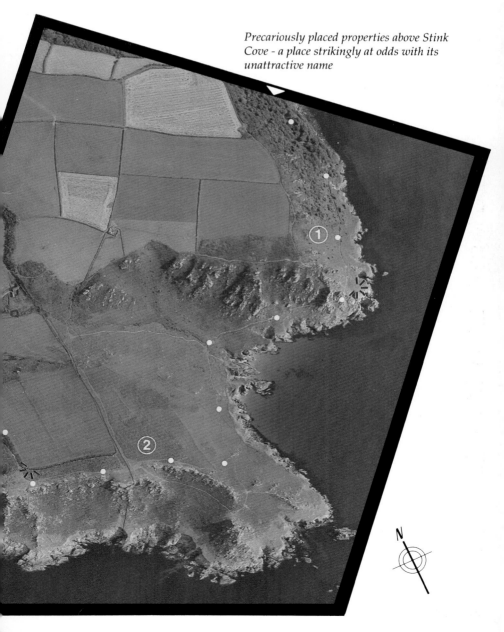

SOAR MILL COVE is a stolen break in the cliffs. Offshore lies another Ham Stone. In 1936 the splendid four-masted barque *Herzogin Cecilie* ran aground here after winning the `Grain Race' from Australia. The crew and some of the cargo of grain were saved, but the vessel later sank after being towed to Starehole Bay below Bolt Head.

Where the ridge of Cathole Cliff runs between a sheer drop to the sea and the inland valleys, the Path takes on the flavour of a mountain route, with rocky outcrops such as Hazel Tor adding to the impression. Ground-clinging plants such as the delightful pink and white stonecrop favour this area, and in early summer the seaward slopes become a blue haze of squill.

The radio masts sprouting on Bolberry Down (ahead) are part of a Decca Navigator relay station which transmits radio signals. The signals are part of the network of co-ordinates used by aircraft and ships, including many local fishing boats.

---

### ROUTE DIRECTIONS

**1.** Descend steeply to Soar Mill Cove. Either follow a path to the left of a pinnacle on the opposite slope, or veer right along a track that winds inland, then go left up a zig-zag track. Both routes merge at the top of the slope.

*2.* Continue along the airy ridge of Cathole Cliff. Keep to the left-hand tracks at junctions to reach a National Trust car park (refreshments are available at the Port Light Hotel).

---

*This Ham Stone - there are several rocks of this name along the coast of South Devon - lies off Soar Mill Cove betwen Bolt Head and Bolt Tail*

CATHOLE CLIFF

**1.** From the car park exit go down a wide track for a few yards, then turn left. At a triple junction take the middle track.

**2.** Follow the path past the distinctive Gray Stone rock pinnacle.

**3.** Continue straight ahead where the path diverges. The right-hand branch goes directly to Hope Cove. At Bolt Tail follow the arrow posts across the turfy ground and go through the Iron Age fortifications.

**4.** From the top of Bolt Tail drop down to the right and follow the path, keeping left at junctions, and go on to Inner Hope.

**5.** Go down past the old lifeboat house and walk along the road above the beach to Outer Hope which has a pub, a shop, telephone, toilets and bus connections. Continue up a surfaced track that starts beyond the Hope and Anchor Inn, then turn left up some steps and on to the Coast Path.

THE EARLY IRON AGE promontory fort on Bolt Tail dates from the period 400BC to AD50. It features, typically, a fortified revetment across the neck of the headland. The fortifications include some dry-stone walls and there are vestigial remains of a ditch.

Hope Cove, with its early settlement of Inner Hope, has had long associations with fishing and smuggling and general seafaring, not least the heroic work of the lifeboat service. There was a lifeboat stationed at Inner Hope from 1877 until 1930 and the surviving lifeboat house bears witness to its great service. Inner Hope also boasts a cluster of sturdy thatched cottages.

*Bolt Tail, site of an Iron Age promontory fort*

*Thurlestone Rock*

③

N

*The two hamlets at Hope Cove — Inner Hope and Outer Hope*

THE OLD VILLAGE of Thurlestone lies hidden behind its modern seaward-facing houses. The name Thurlestone comes from the offshore rock with its distinctive archway. The Saxon word for pierced stone is said to be *torlestan*, which may be the source of the present name, although the dialect word `thirled', meaning `worn through by the wind', may be the source. The Thurlestone Rock was the subject of a typically atmospheric painting by J. M. W. Turner.

Thurlestone village is archetypal Devon. Thatched cottages with flower-filled gardens and climbing plants are complemented by exotic palm trees. The tower of the 12th-century red sandstone church of All Saints was used in the past as an early form of lighthouse, or beacon, through use of a fire-pan.

Walkers should be on the alert for flying golf balls along the extended stretch that borders the Thurlestone golf course. The path passes close to several tees and greens. There are ample warning notices, and a reciprocal courtesy from walkers and golfers is encouraged.

## ROUTE DIRECTIONS

**1.** Go through a gate and down a surfaced lane. Turn left at a T-junction and follow the road, then go through the car park at South Milton Sands.

*2.* Turn left just past a toilet block. Cross South Milton Ley reed bed by a boardwalk and continue to Leasfoot Beach, from where Thurlestone can be reached if desired.

**3.** Follow the path keeping close to the cliff edge with the golf course to the right.

THURLESTONE

IF FERRYING OR FORDING the Avon is not possible, a 10-mile (16km) detour via Aveton Gifford is necessary. The inland path is clearly marked on sheet 1362 of the OS Pathfinder series. Its start is located by following the road from the car park into Bantham to the junction at the Sloop Inn. Take the left fork for several yards and look out for a signpost and track going left. *Note*: once across the road bridge on the approach to Aveton Gifford, turn immediately left down the riverbank road. However, this may be under tidal water requiring a wait or a detour through Aveton Gifford followed by a left turn to cross Waterhead Bridge to reach a link path to Were Down. At low tide, the riverbank road and linking paths and roads can be followed to Bigbury-on-Sea.

ROUTE DIRECTIONS

**1.** Continue to the large car park at Bantham where there are refreshments, toilets, and telephones.

**2.** From the exit to the car park, go down a lane on the left and then down left to the ferry slipway by the thatched boathouse. There is a seasonal ferry service which should be used when available. The Avon can be waded at dead low water, but walkers should consider carefully before doing so especially if carrying heavy rucksacks. The author has waded the Avon comfortably from either side, but conditions were ideal with calm weather, low water of a spring tide when tide levels are at a minimum, and after a dry period. Wading the Avon should not be attempted at any point other than the one described.

**3.** Go along the beach to the right from the boathouse until level with the distinctive turret on the bank above. With the turret behind you, wade the river carefully, keeping in line with the broad row of trees that run uphill from the opposite bank.

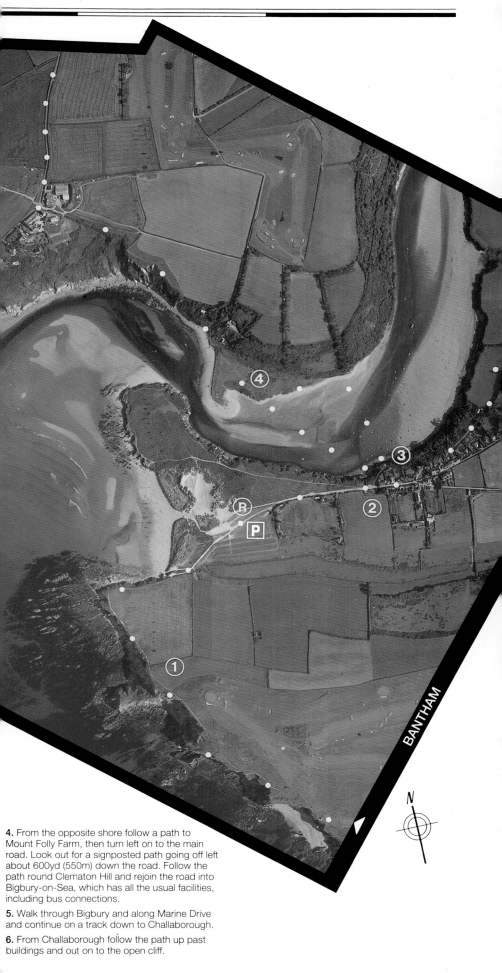

**4.** From the opposite shore follow a path to Mount Folly Farm, then turn left on to the main road. Look out for a signposted path going off left about 600yd (550m) down the road. Follow the path round Clematon Hill and rejoin the road into Bigbury-on-Sea, which has all the usual facilities, including bus connections.

**5.** Walk through Bigbury and along Marine Drive and continue on a track down to Challaborough.

**6.** From Challaborough follow the path up past buildings and out on to the open cliff.

BANTHAM

N

# Bigbury-on-Sea to Noss Mayo

13 miles (20.8km)

**This wonderfully varied section of the Coast Path passes through
some strenuous country before reaching the lovely River Erme.
Judicious timing should make wading the Erme straightforward.
Some further ups and downs lead to Revelstoke Drive which runs
on the level all the way to Noss Mayo.**

BURGH ISLAND, like its much grander
equivalent in Cornwall's Mounts Bay.
was dedicated to St Michael. It is
distinguished by its art deco style hotel
where Agatha Christie wrote two of her
novels. The island can be reached on
foot at low tide, or by a hybrid sea
tractor when the causeway is

*The 28-acre rock known as Burgh Island has welcomed many well-known visitors to its
private hotel over the years*

*Meddrick Rocks, just below the mouth of the Erme estuary*

underwater. The 14th century Pilchard Inn enjoys its offshore status.

The coast between Bigbury and the Erme edges round one of those sweetly remote areas of the South Hams that seems genuinely timeless. Dartmouth slate dominates the cliff landscape where the cliffs gleam as white as the chalk cliffs of Beer. Above one bulging sheet of glossy slate on the western rim of Ayrmer Cove depressions in the turf and signs of a hoist indicate either that seaweed was lifted here for use as a fertiliser or that slate was hoisted for

building. Hoist Point, a short distance further on, was certainly a site for these activities.

## ROUTE DIRECTIONS

**1.** Descend steeply to Ayrmer Cove, cross a bridge and go through tall reeds to continue steeply uphill. Follow the path along a flat-topped cliff edge.

**2.** Descend steeply to Westcombe Beach. A tough climb follows to Hoist Point from where the path takes an undulating course towards The Beacon. It is rather meanly pressed to seaward by a wire fence.

WESTCOMBE BEACH

## ROUTE DIRECTIONS

**1.** Follow the path round Fernycombe Point to Wonwell Beach.

**2.** Cross the inside edge of Wonwell Beach and continue along a path through some trees and on to a road. Turn left and go down to the foreshore. (At low water it is sometimes possible to walk along the seashore from Wonwell Beach to this point.)

There is no ferry service across the River Erme. If the walker does not wish to ford the stream a 9-mile (14.4km) detour is necessary inland to Sequers Bridge on the A379. Better to get your timing right for the ford and your feet nicely cooled in the process.

**3.** It is possible to wade across the Erme from one hour before low water, (preferrably during a spring tide) until one hour after. Dry weather and quiet seas are best. In such ideal conditions the author has waded the Erme two hours before low water with ease, though care should always be exercised if carrying a heavy pack. During neap tides, low water is less generous in its fall. The best line for wading is to start a few yards up river from the end of the foreshore road. Wade on firm ground directly across to the uncovered sand, then continue to the slipway at Mothecombe Beach.

**4.** Walk up the slipway, then go left over a stile and through trees to descend a stepped path to Meadowsfoot Beach.

**5.** Cross the beach if it is low water (an alternative along a causeway is signposted) towards the charming old building, once used as a tea house, and climb the steps. Continue steeply, crossing a stile and passing through woods on to the open cliff to pass above Bugle Hole.

MOTHERCOMBE

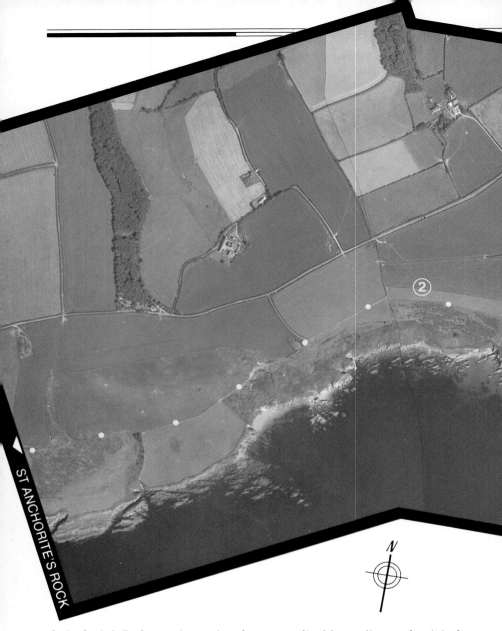

*St Anchorite's Rock, more impressive when seen outlined from a distance than it is close-to.*

THE SERENITY of the Erme estuary and the surrounding countryside of the old Flete Estate has much to do with its history of land ownership. Flete House, which lies embedded amid the quiet beauty of the upper Erme, was owned by a succession of noble names whose benign policy towards the landscape and stout farming traditions have left the area genuinely unspoilt.

The impressive pinnacle of St Anchorite's Rock seems more like a displaced Dartmoor tor than a coastal feature. Its name is said to come from a pinnacle-perching hermit of the `stylite' persuasion, who once roosted there like the birds of prey which favoured its commanding heights. The rock is short-changed on the seaward side, but has an impressive 60ft (18m) back wall which has been quarried.

The strange ruined building on Beacon Hill is recorded on 18th century maps as the Membland Pleasure House. Its precise purpose has not been specified, but it is unlikely to have been the fleshly antithesis of poor old St Anchorite's cold corner. Most likely it was yet another tea house - in the best possible taste.

ROUTE DIRECTIONS

**1.** Continue along the path to pass St Anchorite's Rock, then go down into a dip with a few pine trees.

**2.** Continue through fields keeping towards the coast until in sight of the steep rise of Beacon Hill. Ignore a stile on the left that directs the walker down towards the sea. Instead, keep to the right of the fence running directly ahead. Follow the line of the fence up a merciless incline to reach level ground beside the ruined Membland Pleasure House.

THE RUIN OF THE ancient church of St Peter the Poor Fisherman sits uneasily amid a caravan park, but nevertheless it has a compelling atmosphere and its graveyard is an open book of sad departures.

The sheltered site east of Stoke Point and the complex of small coves fringing the bay would have been exploited at an early stage and there has been a place of worship here since the 13th century at least. There are good views to the east both to seaward and inland and the existing alder wood indicates that this is a well-watered spot.

St Peter's was the parish church of Noss Mayo, which argues a fairly robust flock considering the distance between the two. The church was damaged by storms in 1840 and by 1870 it was declared unsafe. Lord Revelstoke built another church of St Peter in Noss Mayo and the church at Stoke was abandoned.

In the 1960s local efforts secured aid from the Redundant Churches Fund and St Peter's has since been partly restored, although it is still roofless. It remains a consecrated place of worship and seems tangibly so because of its poignant history and strange setting. Occasional services are held.

NOSS MAYO

## ROUTE DIRECTIONS

**1.** Follow Revelstoke Drive to its junction with the road that leads into the caravan park at Stoke House. There is a shop here during the season, and a telephone.

**2.** Go straight across and through a kissing-gate to continue along the wooded drive. (Alternatively, turn left and go down the steep road to the church of St Peter. From beyond the church follow a path leading westward along the cliff edge to rejoin Revelstoke Drive above Swale Cove.)

**3.** Emerge from the trees and continue pleasantly along the grassy drive above Netton Down and Snellings Down.

④

N

A FERRY SERVICE operates between
the landing stage by Ferry Wood, Yealm
Steps on the Newton Ferrers side and
Warren Point. It runs for a limited
period during the main summer season.
Strong lungs and few inhibitions are
needed to summon the ferry from the
Yealm Steps pontoon if it is not closer at
hand. *Do not attempt to wade the Yealm. It
is deep and dangerous.* If the ferry is not
available, offer a quick prayer to
St Christopher and you may find a
generous boat person already afloat.
Otherwise a long detour inland via
Yealmpton is the only option. If this is
the case, walk on to Noss Mayo from
where buses to Plymouth can be taken
and a link made to Wembury.

## ROUTE DIRECTIONS

**1.** Continue past the ruins of Gunrow Signal
Station, a late 18th century watchhouse.

*2.* Follow Revelstoke Drive past Blackstone Point.
(Above the Point a path leads inland to a National
Trust car park. This offers a short cut to Noss
Mayo.)

**3.** Walk past Warren Cottage via a short path
diversion on the left. Continue round Gara Point
and Mouthstone Point.

**4.** Pass some coastguard houses, then continue
through woods past the handsome Battery
Cottage. A path drops down left from here to the
sheltered Cellar Beach.

**5.** Follow a surfaced road through Ferry Wood for
about 400yd (366m), then look out for some
stone steps leading down left to a landing stage.
These are just past a parking bay. Having crossed
to Warren Point, turn left and follow the path uphill.

# Noss Mayo to Turnchapel

7 miles (9.6km)

**The last lap! From the wooded banks of the Yealm to the increasingly urbanised coast the walking is relatively easy. However, there is still much to interest the walker all the way to Turnchapel; not least the ever-widening views of the mighty Plymouth Sound.**

THE REPEATED USE of the name `Warren' along the Coast Path dates back to the last century when rabbits were farmed for their meat and fur. Artificial warrens were created within enclosing walls and the trade of warrener became well established throughout the South West. Even the Great Mew Stone off Wembury Point had its resident warrener in the shape of the notorious Sam Wakeham.

The beach at Wembury has been preserved from unsympathetic development through being in the care of the National Trust. There is a Trust shop and a café housed in the old mill. The most striking feature, however, is the church of St Werburgh, dedicated to Weigenbeorge, the daughter of the 7th century King of Mercia. The church is mainly 15th century although the tower with its prominent stair-tower is earlier. Inside there are finely carved oak rafters with painted motifs and rather handsome monuments to the Calmady and Hele families.

## ROUTE DIRECTIONS

**1.** Turn left at a house by a gate. The gate gives access to Warren Lane which leads to Wembury just over ½mile (800m) inland where there are refreshments, shops, a post office, telephone, toilets and bus connections.

**2.** Follow the path round Season Point.

**3.** At a junction by a bungalow keep straight on and go down to Wembury Beach. Cross the beach, which has a café, a shop and toilets, and continue along the low edge of the cliff.

WEMBURY BEACH

*Wembury's church may have been built on the cliff-top partly to act as a landmark for sailors*

*It is hard to imagine that the Great Mew Stone, off Wembury Point, was inhabited by people at one time*

HMS *CAMBRIDGE* is a contemporary reminder of the strategic importance of this area of Devon. For centuries the Sound was a great naval centre and successive monarchs and governments ringed the coastline to either side with fortifications against the historical enemies, Spain and France. The contrast, from this point on, between the rural peace of the South Hams and the recurring traces of coastal defence, is remarkable.

## ROUTE DIRECTIONS

**1.** Continue along the low cliff edge with open fields on the right.

**2.** At HMS *Cambridge* Gunnery School pay heed to the warning notice. Red flags or red lights on display mean that firing to seaward is in progress. If firing is NOT in progress, continue along the path to seaward of the complex. (Tea breaks or prolonged naps are not advised.)

When firing is under way there is an alternative route through the complex. Turn up right from the warning notice for a short distance, then turn left at the corner by a small-arms firing range and go up a surfaced road. Follow a right branch steeply uphill to a 'yellow spot' roundabout with several roads branching off. Directional signs are ambiguous here. Stay cool and go directly ahead, between buildings. (If red lights are flashing, put your hands over your ears as guns are about to fire.) Continue through a car parking area, then go down a surfaced path.

**3.** Continue down the road to Heybrook Bay with its pub, telephone and bus connections. Turn left at the bottom of the road and walk along in front of bungalows and on to the path above low cliffs. Follow the path round Andurn Point.

*Now an adventure centre, Drake's Island was used as a military fortress from the mid-16th century to 1956*

THE INSPIRING VIEWS across Plymouth Sound from this section of the path explain precisely why Fort Bovisand was established. Bovisand was part of the ring fort system set up round Plymouth Sound by Lord Palmerston at the outbreak of the Napoleonic wars. The fort was matched by Picklecombe Fort on the opposite shore and linked strategically to the fort on Plymouth Breakwater. The man-made cutting crossed by the Coast Path was used for lowering supplies and armoury to Fort Bovisand. The fort is now an Underwater Centre used by a number of organisations.

The solid walls on the skyline were built as a buffer for a late 19th century rifle range connected with Fort Staddon which lies just inland. The wall was designed to look like yet another fort.

There are splendid views of Plymouth Breakwater from the path. A need for a breakwater was recognised as early as the 18th century when Plymouth Sound had become notorious as a bad anchorage in southerly gales. The Breakwater, begun in 1812 but not fully completed until 1841, was carried out by the great Victorian engineer John Rennie who insisted on the `island' design, having recognised that the huge quantities of silt washed down by the Rivers Plym and Tamar would cause a massive build-up of sand and mud if a breakwater was attached to either shore. The Breakwater, just under a mile (1.5km) long, required several million tons of stone.

ROUTE DIRECTIONS

**1.** Walk up through a chalet park at Bovisand. Refreshments, a shop, toilets, telephones and bus connections can all be found here.

**2.** Cross above the beach area, then continue up a steep path. Turn left into a parking area. Veer slightly right in front of the first row of houses to where a flight of slate steps leads up right.

**3.** Turn left at the top of the steps and continue across a wooden footbridge over a man-made cutting. Continue round Staddon Heights through pleasant woods to reach the road.

**4.** Turn left and walk down the often busy road to the café at Jennycliff's southern end.

*Plymouth Breakwater*

IT SEEMS A PITY, after all the marvellous miles of walking from Lyme Regis, that there is neither ferry, ford nor convenient bridge to ease the walker into the heart of Plymouth; or on to Cornwall and the far west. But Turnchapel has lost its ferry and rail link and is at the mercy of the motorcar. It is best left by bus.

In some ways however this official, and emphatic end to the South Devon Coast Path gives time for reflection, and Turnchapel, with its resilient atmosphere of old-Devon-by-the-sea, is

no bad place in which to reflect.

Mount Batten Point has been crucial to Turnchapel's past. The Point was settled in the Iron Age and there is evidence of trading with France from that period. The sea almost claimed Mount Batten as an island when it breached the neck of the Point last century, but it remained locked to the mainland when Plymouth's municipal rubbish was tipped in between.

The strategically-placed small island now called Drake's Island was known in the 12th century as St Michael's Island,

when it belonged to the priors of
Plympton. By 1550 the first defences
were erected and soon after, Sir Francis
Drake was appointed governor and the
island was renamed St Nicholas, before
the more obvious present name was
adopted. It went through a turbulent
history of siege and defence, became a
prison in the 17th century and then
played a key part in Plymouth's defences
right through to the Second World War.
The island is now in the hands of the
National Trust and is leased to the City
of Plymouth as an adventure centre.

## ROUTE DIRECTIONS

**1.** The main road can be followed directly to
Turnchapel where the South Devon Coast Path
ends. There are bus connections from here to
Plymouth. Alternatively, walk down the grassy
open space of Jennycliff Field, then continue
round Dunstone Point.

**2.** Go on to the road by Fort Stamford, then turn
left by the entrance to Mount Batten and go down
St John's Road and so to the waterfront at
Turnchapel.

# PLYMOUTH

Devon's great maritime city has survived the rumours and rigours of war for centuries. It is now the county's largest urban area and has spread inland well beyond its historic waterfront. The city evolved through the amalgamation of Sutton harbour, Stonehouse on the west and Dock, which later became Devonport, on the Hamoaze where the Tamar enters the Sound.

The original port at Sutton was of little significance until the great maritime adventures of the 16th century, when it became strategically best-placed for westward maritime exploration. There are 40 Plymouths worldwide. The city's naval dockyards have been its life, but Plymouth has evolved independently as an impressive conurbation and as the urban focus for Devon and Cornwall. Although heavily bombed during the last war, it has emerged with vigour and with its identity intact. The famous limestone height of Plymouth Hoe is like an open invitation to set sail, poised as it is above the Sound. But not before the city is explored for its many delights.

The Hoe is essentially a magnificent promenade, which should recommend it to coastal walkers, however footsore they may be. The Marine Biological Association's splendid aquarium is at the eastern end of the Hoe on Citadel Hill. So too is the Royal Citadel, first laid out in the mid-16th century on even older foundations, The Citadel was largely rebuilt in neo-Gothic style in the 1840s and remains one of the city's most impressive buildings. There are conducted tours of the interior at set times.

The Barbican area of the old town retains much of Plymouth's historic character. It lies to the north of the Hoe on the west side of Sutton harbour and is a delightful maze of old streets and alley-ways; some, like the cobbled New Street, date from Elizabethan times. Merchants' houses of the late 16th century are well-preserved and in St Andrew's Street the Merchant's House Museum with its solid walls and timbered front is a delight. The Prysten House in Finewell Street is the city's oldest surviving building and is open to the public. It dates from the 15th

*Devon's largest conurbation is magnificently situated between the Tamar and Plym estuaries*

*Brunel's Royal Albert Bridge carries the railway across the Tamar. Alongside is the Tamar Bridge*

century and has an impressive simplicity of design. A thriving and busy fishing harbour and a yacht marina add to the area's appeal, as do the numerous excellent pubs and restaurants.

Beyond the Barbican and the waterfront the rebuilding of central Plymouth after bomb devastation has produced a spacious and open city, in keeping with the theme of the great Sound and the greater sea beyond.

# Index

Index to places along the South Devon Coast Path

# Useful Organisations

The following bodies may be contacted at the addresses given for any further information required.

Countryside Commission, John Dower House, Crescent Place, Cheltenham, Gloucestershire GL50 3RA

Forestry Commission, 231 Corstorphine Road, Edinburgh EH12 7AT

National Trust, 36 Queen Anne's Gate, London SW1H 9AS

English Nature, Northminster House, Peterborough, Cambridgeshire PE1 1UA

English Heritage, Spur 17, Government Buildings, Hawkenbury, Tunbridge Wells, Kent TN2 5AQ

Long Distance Walkers' Association, 9 Tainters Brook, Hempsted Fields, Uckfield, East Sussex TN22 1UQ

Ramblers' Association, 1/5 Wandsworth Road, London SW8

Youth Hostels Association, Trevelyan House, 8 St Stephens Hill, St Albans, Herts AL1 2DY

West Country Tourist Board, 60 St David's Hill, Exeter EX4 4SY

Devon Wildlife Trust, 35 New Bridge Street, Exeter EX3 4AH

*Brixham harbour*